BATHROO[M]
of
SASKATCHEWAN
TRIVIA

Weird, Wacky and Wild

Glenda MacFarlane

BLUE
BIKE
BOOKS

The Publisher: Blue Bike Books

Library and Archives Canada Cataloguing in Publication

MacFarlane, Glenda
    Bathroom book of Saskatchewan trivia : weird, wacky and wild /
Glenda MacFarlane.

ISBN-13: 978-1-897278-27-7
ISBN-10: 1-897278-27-6

    1. Saskatchewan—Miscellanea. I. Title.

FC3511.M33 2007   971.24   C2007-901524-7

Project Director: Nicholle Carrière
Project Editor: Kathy van Denderen
Production: Jodene Draven
Cover Image: © 2007 Jupiter Images Corporation
Illustrations: Peter Tyler, Roger Garcia, Roly Wood, Graham Johnson

We acknowledge the support of the Alberta Foundation for the Arts for our publishing program.

PC: P5

DEDICATION

To my parents, Sharon and Scotty MacFarlane, with love and thanks.

ACKNOWLEDGEMENTS

First, thank you to my mother, Sharon, and to my brother, Fraser, for all of their suggestions and research help—it's wonderful to have other writers in the family! An enormous thank you to the amazing Dave Geary for sharing his expertise, stories and sources. And thanks to the people of Beechy who rallied around the cause. There really is no place like home.

I'm grateful to everyone who helped me with specific items, including Roxane Schury, Edward Stockman, Donna Redmond, Lois Meaden, Larry Warwaruk, Verna Allinson, Rose Fritz, Penny Barr, Lars Bjorgan, Harold Gates, Teresa Stroeder, the Revisionists Writers' Group, and the fabulous women of Coffee Row, among others.

Thanks also to Lee Gowan, Judith Roback of Toronto's Spadina Library and her husband Richard Chambers, Daryl Demoskoff of Tourism Saskatchewan, Rose-Marie Carey of Batoche National Historic Site, The Arrogant Worms, Kate Newman of Tundra Books, Jeff O'Brien of the City of Saskatoon Archives, Sue Miner, Marina Endicott, Sheila Alianak, Dave Carley, John and Bev Ellis and Camille Marcotte.

Thanks to Leslie French for babysitting while I worked! And of course, special thank-yous go to Faye Boer; to my editor, Kathy van Denderen; and to Nicholle Carrière and all the folks at Blue Bike Books.

Finally, thanks to David French and Mary MacFarlane French for their inspiration and support.

CONTENTS

INTRODUCTION

Prepare to be amazed by some of the things you'll read about in *The Bathroom Book of Saskatchewan Trivia*. Canada's ninth province is home to fewer than a million people, but what we lack in numbers, we make up for in ingenuity, talent and sheer gumption. Many "Skatchies" are outstanding athletes. A substantial number are award-winning authors, heroes or innovators. And a few have done things that will make your hair stand on end!

My grandparents, Ernest and Anna May Handley, were great storytellers. Over the years at their supper table, I heard hundreds of Saskatchewan stories—tales of eccentric homesteaders, rum-runners, hardscrabble farmers, travelling doctors, trappers and politicians. These characters and many more found their way into the pages of this book. Joni Mitchell and Gordie Howe are here, along with a man who built a mechanical horse, and one of Sun Yat-Sen's bodyguards. There's a spy, a Nobel Prize winner in chemistry, and Tommy Douglas. You'll find a good portion of the cast of *Corner Gas,* a giant, a really brave goat, and more than enough ghosts and aliens.

For a sparsely populated jurisdiction in the centre of a large country, Saskatchewan is often ahead of the curve, politically, scientifically and artistically. And of course, we do have noteworthy weather, a vast array of giant roadside attractions, unusual ways of getting things done and a sense of humour about it all.

It's said that there are only two types of people in the world: those who come from Saskatchewan, and those who wish they did. But whether you're a genuine Skatchie or an honorary one, I hope you have as much fun reading this book as I did researching and writing it.

Oh—and Go Roughriders!

ON THE MAP

And now here it is: everything you wanted to know about Saskatchewan, but were afraid to ask! Some essential facts and figures for the "Land of Living Skies"…

Happy Birthday, Dear Saskatchewan…

Saskatchewan was created on September 1, 1905, making it Canada's ninth province. The bouncing baby province was formed by joining parts of the districts of Saskatchewan, Athabasca and Assiniboia. In 2005, Saskatchewan celebrated its centennial with thousands of homecoming parties and special events.

Almost Buffaloed

If it hadn't been for the objections of Clifford Sifton, Canada's minister of the interior, both Saskatchewan and Alberta would have established French as their official language. And Frederick Haultain, premier of the Northwest Territories in 1905, wanted to make Alberta and Saskatchewan into one big province named "Buffalo."

Stop and Ask for Directions

Saskatchewan is in western Canada, located between the provinces of Manitoba and Alberta. To the south lie Montana and North Dakota, to the north is the Northwest Territories (and farther north, Nunavut). The east and west boundaries are 102 and 110 degrees longitude west of the Greenwich meridian. The south and north borders are 49 and 60 degrees latitude north of the equator.

Quadrilateral Power

Saskatchewan is the only province with boundaries not based on any particular geographical features. (This makes it by far the easiest province to draw.)

Green, Gold and Blue

Saskatchewan covers 651,900 square kilometres. Half of the province is covered by forest, one-third is farmland and one-eighth is fresh water. Of the 10 provinces, Saskatchewan ranks fifth in land area.

Ecozones

Saskatchewan is divided into four ecozones: prairie, boreal plains, boreal shield and taiga shield. The Saskatchewan prairie is the largest grassland area in Canada.

The Name Game

The name "Saskatchewan" is a variation on the Cree word "kisiskaciwan," which means "swiftly flowing water." It referred to the South Saskatchewan River.

And Speaking of Water

Although Saskatchewan is a "land-locked" province, it has plenty of H_2O. There are four major river systems: the North Saskatchewan, the South Saskatchewan, the Assiniboine and the Churchill. All empty into Hudson Bay. The province also has 100,000 lakes!

It's Not All Flat, You Know

The highest point of land in Saskatchewan is in the Cypress Hills. At 1468 metres above sea level, the area is the highest point of elevation between the Rockies and Labrador.

POPULATION FACTS

Magic Million

Saskatchewan's population usually hovers just below one million.
At last count (2001), the population was 995,381.

Citified

More than half (about 64 percent) of Saskatchewan's population
lives in cities. The capital city is Regina, with a metropolitan
population of 202,076. The largest city is Saskatoon, population
239,602. The next largest cities are Prince Albert, Moose Jaw,
Yorkton, Swift Current, North Battleford, Estevan and Weyburn.
(Of course, there's also Lloydminster, which straddles the
Alberta/Saskatchewan border. Almost 8000 people live on
the Skatchie side.)

Country Living

If you were paying attention, you'll know by now that about 36 percent of the population lives in rural areas. Saskatchewan has 298 rural municipalities, 376 villages and 146 towns.

Down on the Farm

Approximately 65 million acres of the province is farmland. Saskatchewan accounts for 20 percent of Canada's farms and has the biggest spreads in the country, too, with an average farm size of 1283 acres. The province has nearly 40 percent of the agricultural land in Canada. Other top industries include oil and gas, mining, forestry and tourism.

It Takes All Kinds

Saskatchewan is culturally diverse and includes large populations of people with Aboriginal, British, European, Russian, and Ukrainian heritage.

GOVERNMENT AND SYMBOLS

Governing Bodies

The province has an appointed lieutenant-governor who represents the Crown, a premier, and a unicameral legislature.

Timely

Saskatchewan stays on Central Standard Time all year round—it's the only province that doesn't have to "spring forward" or "fall back." Not that this policy is without controversy. Logically, Saskatchewan should observe Mountain Standard Time. At one point, municipalities were allowed to choose their own time zone. This resulted in lame jokes, such as, "I went into town to work and got there before I left home."

DID YOU KNOW?

"SK" is the official abbreviation for the province. All Saskatchewan postal codes start with the letter "S."

Blooming Marvellous

The western red lily was named the official flower of Saskatchewan in 1941. The blazing red-orange blossoms grow in semi-wooded areas and meadows. Once abundant, the western red lily is now a protected species.

Just Us Chickens

Saskatchewan's official bird is the sharp-tailed grouse, which is often referred to by flatlanders (mistakenly) as the "prairie chicken." A female sharp-tailed grouse lays her eggs in a shallow hole lined with grasses and soft leaves. The birds are known for their colourful courtship displays.

Button Up Your Coat of Arms

The provincial Coat of Arms was granted through Royal Warrant by Queen Elizabeth II in 1986, an augmentation of the 1906 Coat of Arms. It shows a beaver and a crown above a shield. On either side of the shield are a royal lion and a deer. The shield itself depicts a lion and three wheat sheaves, symbolizing agriculture. It has a base of western red lilies.

Motto

The Coat of Arms also features the provincial motto *Multis E Gentibus Vires,* which means, appropriately, "From Many Peoples Strength."

But What Do We Wear Under It?

Saskatchewan's provincial tartan was registered with the Court of Lord Lyon, King of Arms in Scotland in 1961. It features seven colours: gold for prairie wheat, brown for the summerfallow, green for the forests, red for the western red lily, yellow for the canola flower and the sunflower, white for snow, and black for coal and oil. Unfortunately, there is no official Saskatchewan haggis recipe yet.

Flag-Waving

The top half of Saskatchewan's flag is green, representing the forested north. The bottom half is as golden as a field of wheat, symbolizing southern grain farming. The flag also features the provincial shield of arms and the western red lily.

Son of a Birch

The provincial tree is the white birch, a versatile and beautiful hardwood tree that is found throughout northern Saskatchewan.

Deer Me

Saskatchewan's official animal is the white-tailed deer, which has a reddish-brown summer coat and a greyish-brown winter coat. The deer's name comes from the white underside of its tail, which flips up when the animal is running or jumping over fences.

Green, Green Grass of Home

Needle-and-thread grass is Saskatchewan's official grass. The native bunchgrass sports a pointy seed with long, thready fibres attached to it.

A Mess o' Potash

Potash (sylvite) is the province's official mineral. Saskatchewan is the world's largest producer and exporter of potash, which is used mainly for fertilizer.

Hurry Hard

In 2001, curling was named Saskatchewan's official sport.

WILD WEATHER

When most Canadians hear the words "Saskatchewan" and "weather" in the same sentence, the usual reaction is "Brrr." And it's true that in Saskatchewan, winter is in a class of its own. Ask any Saskatchewan kid to describe the agony of a tongue frozen to a flagpole. Open the trunk of any car with Saskatchewan plates and you'll find a set of jumper cables inside. But winter isn't the only meteorological story in Saskatchewan.

Dirty Thirties

☛ During the Great Depression of 1929–38, hail and drought devastated Saskatchewan's farm-based economy. Dust storms lasted for days at a time during the worst years of the drought. One day in January 1931, a time of year better known for snow blizzards, it was impossible to see across the street in Moose Jaw due to blowing dust.

☛ The hottest temperature ever recorded in Canada occurred during the height of the Depression: On July 5, 1937, the mercury in both Midale and Yellowgrass hit the 45°C mark. At that temperature steel railway lines begin to twist, and fruit on trees starts to cook.

☛ Other periods of extreme drought in Saskatchewan happened in the mid-1960s and the late '80s. And although agricultural practices have alleviated some of the problems that occurred in the '30s, central Saskatchewan still has the second-highest annual dust-storm frequency in North America.

RAIN, HAIL AND FLOODING

On the Other Hand

In July 2000, 300 millimetres of rain poured down on the community of Vanguard in one eight-hour period. Every road leading into the village was either destroyed or rendered impassable.

Looking on the Bright Side

On August 3, 1985, 380 millimetres of rain fell on Parkman. Two brothers decided to find the silver lining despite their drowned crops—they went water-skiing on their wheatfield.

Rainmakers

Weather Modification, Inc., a Denver-based company, came to Saskatoon in 1954. Their professed aim was to encourage Mother Nature to produce rain by spraying chemicals into the air currents. When a deluge of rain fell in the Borden area the following year, angry farmers practically ran the company out of town.

What the Hail?!

On August 11, 1972, severe thunderstorms ravaged southeastern Saskatchewan. Canada's largest hailstone fell that day near Cedoux. It measured 10 centimetres in diameter and weighed 290 grams—about as much as a can of soup!

DID YOU  **KNOW?**

In May 1961, hailstones as large as chicken eggs fell on the hamlet of Buffalo Gap. The hail piled up more than one metre deep in some places.

Get Out Your Floodpants

In the spring of 1996, temperatures rose by 20 degrees in three days, melting an above-average accumulation of snow a little too quickly. Thousands of sandbags were piled along Wascana Creek to combat the resulting flooding in Regina.

WIND

Gone with the Wind

In August 1944, an F-4 tornado hit Kamsack. One woman was killed when a freight car was hurled through the window of the Canadian National Railway (CNR) station. Two others also died, and damage was extensive.

Blowhard

A tornado that hit Peebles in July 1989 blew the general store and the curling rink into the bush—landing about 3 kilometres from where they'd originally stood.

Double Whammy

That same year, eight tornadoes with wind gusts of up to 130 kilometres per hour hit central Saskatchewan. In Blaine Lake, a tornado was followed by a shower of crop-destroying hail.

Insurance Premiums Must Be High in Pilot Butte
In August 1995, thunderstorms accompanied by 100-kilometre-per-hour winds and hail tore through Pilot Butte, where trees were stripped bare and every single property in the 440-home village sustained some damage.

Canada's Worst Tornado

On June 30, 1912, as residents got ready for Dominion Day celebrations, an F-4 tornado with wind speeds over 300 kilometres per hour ripped through Regina. The tornado, referred to as the "Regina Cyclone," only lasted three minutes, but 28 people were killed and 300 were injured. Another 2500 were left homeless when 514 of the Queen City's wooden buildings were flattened.

Dip, Dip and Fly

When the 1912 Regina Cyclone hit, 12-year old Bruce Langton and a friend were canoeing on Wascana Lake. Suddenly the funnel lifted the canoe out of the water. Langton's companion was hurled to the ground and killed, but Langton himself was deposited—canoe and all—in a park hundreds of metres away. When he landed, Langton was still clutching his paddle.

A Different Sort of Horror Show

An actor named William Henry Pratt was in Regina with a touring theatre company on the day of the 1912 disaster. Although the hotel he was staying at was decimated, Pratt remained in the city and organized a benefit concert, with proceeds going to victims of the cyclone. The actor later changed his name to "Boris Karloff" and became famous—as the monster in the Hollywood movie *Frankenstein*.

COLD AND SNOW

Yes, But it's a Dry Cold

Saskatchewan is the driest province in Canada. The lowest temperature recorded in the province is -56.7°C at Prince Albert in 1893. Cold weather can also last a while, as evidenced by the 129-day cold snap (temperatures below -10°C) in several communities during the winter of 1955–56.

Back in Ought-Seven...

And of course, there's the legendary winter of 1906–07, when extreme cold and a series of blizzards wreaked havoc. Nearly 70 percent of range cattle in southwest Saskatchewan perished.

Blizzards

Saskatchewan's most notorious weather event, the blizzard, is defined as four or more hours of intense windchill, strong winds (40 or more kilometres per hour) and enough blinding snow to reduce visibility to one kilometre or less. Blizzards are more prevalent in the southern half of the province. Regina and Swift Current average 30 blizzard-hours per year, while Saskatoon gets only about six. The average duration of a blizzard is 12 hours.

Stormy Weather

☞ A series of blizzards plagued the province in 1947. For 10 days in February all highways into Regina were blocked. Railway officials declared conditions the worst in Canadian rail history. One train was buried in a snowdrift one kilometre long and 8 metres deep. And one farmer tried to get to his barn to milk the cows, but snow blocked the barn door. He had to cut a hole in the roof and climb through!

☞ December 1955: A 26-hour blizzard rocked Saskatchewan with winds blasting 121 kilometres per hour. Two people died, including one RCMP officer.

☞ January 1973: Fifteen hours of blizzard with 84-kilometre-per-hour winds shut down many communities.

☞ February 1978: A four-day blizzard paralyzed much of southern Saskatchewan. In many communities, snowdrifts reached the rooftops.

☞ January 2007: A blizzard blasted central Saskatchewan, with temperatures dipping well below -30°C, 90-kilometre-per-hour winds and 25 centimetres of snow. In Saskatoon, emergency personnel used snowmobiles to reach people trapped in snowbound vehicles. At least three people died after leaving their cars.

MISCELLANEOUS

Vitamin D Overload

Estevan gets the most sunshine of any location in Canada, with an average of 2510 sunshiny hours per year, and an all-time record of 2701 hours. The province itself is Canada's sunniest jurisdiction.

Going to Extremes
Saskatchewan, far from the influence of oceans and mountains, experiences a large range of temperatures each day. And its annual ranges in temperature are the greatest of any of the provinces.

Some Other Records
- *Greatest snowfall:*   Pelly, 386 centimetres in 1955–56
- *Most blowing snow days:*   Moose Jaw, 65 days in 1973–74
- *Most fog days:*   Collins Bay, 61 days in 1980
- *Most thunder days:*   Beechy, 54 days in 1977
- *Longest wet period:*   Whitesand, 180 days in 1978

And Some Other Natural Phenomena

- Saskatchewan is a great place to view the aurora borealis, or northern lights—the phenomenon the First Nations once called "the pathway to heaven."

- The strongest earthquake in Saskatchewan happened in the spring of 1909. The quake was felt from Winnipeg to Lethbridge, and from Prince Albert to St. Paul, Minnesota. Luckily, it caused only minor damage.

TIMELINE

From prehistoric algae to centennial celebrations, it's been a wild ride. Here are some of Saskatchewan's historical highlights:

10,000 BC: First evidence of early peoples

8000 BC: Glaciers retreat; Saskatchewan starts to become grassland

2100 BC: Humans from the American high plains move into what is now Saskatchewan

1530 AD: The first European goods make their way to the prairies, brought by Aboriginal people from the south

1670: Hudson's Bay Co. gets rights to Rupert's Land

1691: Henry Kelsey meets with Plains Natives

1730s: French build trading posts along Saskatchewan River; first appearance of horses in the area

1754: Anthony Henday comes to the plains

1774: Cumberland House established by Hudson's Bay Co.

1792: Hudson's Bay Co. at Fort Carlton

1821: Northwest Co. merges with HBC; a handful of Christian missionaries and farmers make their way into the region

1820s Metis begin to make their mark as a major economic and military force in the west

1850: Fur trade begins to decline

1857: Captain Palliser investigates the area

1867: British North America Act, Confederation

1869:   Rupert's Land sold to federal government

1870:   Homesteaders begin to arrive

1871–77:   Seven treaties negotiated with Plains First Nations

1872:   Federal government establishes residential schools
           for Native children

1873:   Cypress Hills massacre

1874:   North West Mounted Police (NWMP) arrive on
           the "March West"

1875:   Northwest Territories Act provides a mechanism
           for governing the areas that would become
           Saskatchewan and Alberta

1876:   Sitting Bull comes to Wood Mountain

1878:   First public school opened in Battleford

1880:   Last sighting of a significant buffalo herd; a way of
           life has ended

1882:   Telegraph lines reach Regina, or "Pile o' Bones" as
           it is originally dubbed

1885:   Northwest Rebellion

1887:   First MP elected from the region; only white males
           can vote

1888:   First legislative assembly

1890s: Commercial mining of lignite coal begins in the
           Estevan area

1896:   Clifford Sifton encourages settlers

1900:   Territorial Grain Growers Association is created,
           the first of many co-operative organizations

1901–02:   Population explosion: Saskatchewan's population increases by 440 percent in one year

1905:   Saskatchewan becomes a province; the following year Regina is named its capital

1906:   56,000 farms exist in Saskatchewan, producing 50 million bushels of grain

1907:   First municipally-owned hospital in western Canada, in Saskatoon

1909:   Construction begins on University of Saskatchewan

1910:   The Regina Rugby Club, forerunner of the Roughriders, is formed

1911:   Marquis wheat introduced

1912:   Regina Cyclone hits; Saskatchewan's legislative building is officially opened in Regina

1914–18:   World War I

1914:   Daylight Savings Time is tried for the first time in Saskatchewan, and abandoned weeks later…and the debate goes on…

1916:   Women get the right to vote

1918:   Influenza epidemic kills thousands

1919:   First minimum wage legislation passed

1920:   RCMP moves its headquarters to Regina

1921:   Prohibition begins; the Farmers Union is formed

1924:   Saskatchewan Wheat Pool formed; Prohibition is repealed

1927:   The Ku Klux Klan holds a huge rally in Moose Jaw

1928:   Largest harvest on record: Saskatchewan produces 40 percent of the world's wheat supply

1929:   The League of Indians of Western Canada is formed

1929–37:   Great Depression hits the Prairies

1931:   Relief Commission established; coal miners strike near Estevan

1932:   Lowest price (39¢ per bushel) for wheat on the world market in 300 years

1933:   The Regina Manifesto

1934:   Liberals are elected—Conservatives fail to win a single seat

1935:   Regina Riot; Prairie Farm Rehabilitation Act; Canadian Wheat Board established

1936:   School of art founded by Augustus Kenderdine

1937:	Regina Hebrew Savings and Credit Union becomes first credit union in the province
1939–45:	World War II
1944:	Co-operative Commonwealth Federation (CCF) elected; first commercial oil well begins production near Lloydminster; Trade Union Act passed
1946:	Potash mining begins; the Union of Saskatchewan Indians formed
1947:	W.O. Mitchell writes *Who Has Seen the Wind*; hospital insurance plan introduced
1949:	Government begins rural electrification
1950–53:	Korean War
1952:	Uranium production in Saskatchewan begins
1954:	RCAF trainer collides with a passenger plane above Moose Jaw, 37 people die
1957:	John Diefenbaker, first prime minister from Saskatchewan, is elected
1958:	Federation of Saskatchewan Indians formed
1959:	First computer arrives in Saskatchewan
1962:	Medicare introduced; doctors strike
1964:	Liberals win election
1966:	Roughriders win Grey Cup for first time
1967:	Gardiner Dam opens
1968:	Prince Albert Pulp Mill opens
1971:	New Democratic Party (NDP) regain power, several Crown corporations created

1976:   Saskatchewan Indian Federation College holds its first classes

1980s: Rural depopulation intensifies

1982:   Conservatives win election for the first time since 1929

1984:   Changes to Crow Rate

1991:   NDP elected

1992:   Heavy oil upgrader built in Lloydminster; Wanuskewin Heritage Park opens

1994:   T-Rex fossil found near Eastend; no-fault auto insurance introduced

1996:   Scandal in Conservative Party leads to fraud charges against former members of PC caucus

1997:   Saskatchewan Party formed

1998:   Sandra Schmirler curling team and speedskater Catriona LeMay Doan win Olympic gold

2003:   "Mad cow disease" scare devastates the cattle industry

2004:   Canadian Light Synchotron opens; same-sex marriage becomes legal; Canadians choose Tommy Douglas as "Greatest Canadian"

2005:   Saskatchewan celebrates 100 years as a province

FAUNA

Here's a glimpse at some of Saskatchewan's residents...

Duck, Duck, Goose...and Other Birds

☛ Saskatchewan is sometimes known as "North America's Duck Factory." Almost one in four ducks on the continent is raised in the province.

☛ There's a major bird flyway over the province. In the spring or fall, over 2 million ducks and geese stop off as they wing their way between Texas and the Arctic.

☛ The largest bird breeding population of any basin in North America occurred in 1996 at Big Quill Lake, which attracted 7.9 percent of the continental population.

☛ Last Mountain Lake National Wildlife Area is the continent's oldest bird sanctuary, established in 1887. Endangered whooping cranes pass through the area as they migrate.

☛ Redberry Lake and its islands support about 200 species of birds, including American white pelicans.

☛ The Saskatchewan Burrowing Owl Interpretive Centre is home to endangered wild burrowing owls during the summer.

Unofficial Emblem

Although the Western Meadowlark is not Saskatchewan's official bird, the small songbird with the yellow breast is often associated with the province. Perched on fenceposts and road signs, meadowlarks greet the spring with a loud, clear, melodic warble. Some people think they're singing, "I'm a very pretty bird, see my yellow petticoat."

And Other Critters

☞ Common animals in the southern part of the province include elk, grouse, pronghorn antelope and white-tailed deer. And of course, gophers.

☞ A pronghorn antelope can reach speeds of up to 100 kilometres per hour.

☞ The northern half of the province is home to moose, beaver, black bear, wolves and river otters.

☞ Almost 50 percent of the wild boars found in Canada are in Saskatchewan.

☞ In 1999, a polar bear was spotted in Saskatchewan, 400 kilometres from its usual habitat.

☞ Saskatchewan has at least 500 different species of spider.

☞ There are 80 different species of grasshopper in the province.

☞ The only place in Canada where prairie dogs can be found is in southern Saskatchewan near Val Marie, where a colony of black-tailed prairie dogs co-exists with rattlesnakes—they sometimes share burrows!

☞ The most common snake in the province is the garter snake; the only poisonous snake is the prairie rattlesnake.

HUMANS

Way Back on the Family Tree

A campfire and other debris found near Ponteix was estimated to be 10,000 years old. Another site, about 9000 years old, was found near Prelate. Spear tips were discovered there, along with buffalo bones.

We're Number Six!

With a population of 995,381, Saskatchewan is Canada's sixth most-populous province. The highest ranking the province ever enjoyed was in the late 1920s, when the Skatch had the third-largest population.

Rock of Ages

Saskatchewan has more seniors than any other province—15 percent of its residents are over the age of 65. The province also has a slightly higher-than-average population of people 20 and under. The median age is 36.7, just below the national average.

New Home

Seven percent of Saskatchewan residents 15 and older were born outside Canada. Another 22 percent have at least one parent who was born outside the country.

DID YOU KNOW?

There are 94 different ethnic groups represented in the province.

Our Home and Native Land

Thirteen percent of residents identify themselves as Aboriginal, an increase of 17 percent over the past decade. The population of northern Saskatchewan is almost 80 percent Aboriginal, and currently close to half of all children entering school in the province are Aboriginal.

First Nations

First Nations in Saskatchewan are:

☛ Plains Cree (Nehiyawak)

☛ Salteaux (Nahkawininiwak)

☛ Assiniboine (Nakota)

☛ Dakota and Lakota (Sioux)

☛ Dene/Chipewyan (Denesuline)

Métis
A sixth group is the Métis, people of Aboriginal and European descent. Approximately 80,000 people are believed to be part of Saskatchewan's Métis Nation.

Spoken Word
Cree is the most commonly spoken Aboriginal language in Saskatchewan, with about 20,000 Skatchie Cree-speakers. This makes it the second most common language in the province, after English. Cree bands make up over half of the 74 First Nations in Saskatchewan.

Go West!
Following an aggressive campaign to settle the West, by 1911, almost 50 percent of the province's 492,000 residents were immigrants. It was a "man's world," though—67 percent of the population was male, and only 33 percent female—148 men to every 100 women.

Bring on Those Sheepskin Coats

Unlike other provinces, Saskatchewan is neither mostly British nor mostly French. Along with the British and the French, it was settled by many other ethnic groups, including Germans, Ukrainians, Scandinavians, Hungarians and Poles. This influx of immigrants was due in large part to Laurier's Minister of the Interior Clifford Sifton, who famously said, "I think a stalwart peasant in a sheepskin coat, born on the soil, whose forefathers have been farmers for ten generations, with a stout wife and a half-dozen children is good quality."

New Skatchies

Recent arrivals to Saskatchewan are likely to come from farther east. Forty-two percent of immigrants in the past decade have come from Asia, mainly China and the Philippines. Eleven percent of new Saskatchewanians came from the United States, 9 percent from the former Yugoslavia and 4 percent from South Africa. There are fewer than 50,000 immigrants currently living in the province.

Cheers
The largest proportion of settlers in the province came from Britain. Some established utopian colonies, such as the Barr Colony, Cannington Manor, and the York Farmers' Society. Many homesteaders of British stock came from Ontario, including the Temperance Colonists, who settled Saskatoon.

Santé!

A francophone resident of Saskatchewan is known as a "Fransaskois," and early settlers included francophone Métis, migrants from Québec (some of whom were Acadian), plus Europeans from France, Belgium and Switzerland. Francophones established 32 settlements and more than 100 parishes in the province.

Prost!
Today the descendants of German immigrants outnumber any other ethnic group in the province. Mennonites and Hutterites number among the Germans with religious affiliations who came to Saskatchewan.

Skål!

Scandinavian settlers arrived from the U.S. as well as from the "old country." Norwegians were the most numerous, and they arrived early on. Some Finns emigrated twice—they went back to their homeland to set up Red Finland in Karelia, then returned to Saskatchewan when the social experiment failed.

Budmo!

During Clifford Sifton's campaign to settle the West, 170,000 Ukrainians came to Saskatchewan. They've had a big impact on the culture of the province—Premier Roy Romanow, Governor General Ray Hnatyshyn, and Supreme Court Justice John Sopinka all have Ukrainian backgrounds. The University of Saskatchewan offers an M.A. in Slavic Studies, the first of its kind in Canada.

Spirit Wrestlers

In 1899, with help from the Russian novelist Leo Tolstoy and the Quakers, 7400 Doukhobors immigrated from Russia to Canada, where they were given 750,000 acres of land, most of it in Saskatchewan. Doukhobors were pacifists and vegetarians who lived communally; they established 60 communities in the province.

In 1907, demand for land and fear of Doukhobor "communism" led the government to renege on many promises; they tried to force the settlers to fulfill standard homestead requirements and swear allegiance to the Crown. About a thousand independents took up farms, but some demonstrated—in the nude—and others had to be removed from their land. Eventually, 5000 followed their leader, Peter Veregin, to BC.

Friction on the Farmstead

In the mid-1930s, a group of about 30 German families who homesteaded between Meadow Lake and Loon Lake began listening to Goebbels and Hitler via shortwave radio. Eventually, the German families formed their very own German Bund and wanted to be allowed to return to Germany. When the German army took over the Sudetanland, many Czech families fled to England. The enterprising Brits then came up with a solution for the displaced Czechs and the homesick Bund members—they'd deport the Germans and send some Czechs to Canada to take over the Bund farms. However, travel arrangements weren't well thought out, and the Czechs arrived before the Germans had vacated! For a period of time each farm had both a German family and a Czech family living on it, and a great deal of animosity ensued. Finally the Germans departed for the Fatherland—except for the Bund leader, who was sent to an Allied detention camp.

The Colony
In 1949, the first Hutterites came to Saskatchewan and established colonies. Hutterites live communally in groups of about 100. They have unique dress, converse in an archaic German dialect and live an orderly lifestyle—meals are prepared and eaten together, chores are assigned and a (male) member of the colony acts as "Boss." Although they often sell produce in the local area, Hutterites live apart from surrounding farmer families and communities.

Keep on Dancing
Other significant immigrant settlements include Jewish communities near Wapella, Lebanese in Swift Current, and also Dutch, Polish, Hungarians, Czechs and Slovaks, Croatians and Serbs, and Romanians, among others. More recent immigrants include American draft resisters, Vietnamese "boat people" and Chilean refugees. A list of folk dance classes available in the province shows the diverse culture: classes include everything from Balkan to Zydeco to Morris to Scottish to Irish to Israeli!

Runnin' Back to Saskatoon

Between 2000 and 2005, nearly 64,000 Saskatchewan residents moved to Alberta in search of greener economic pastures. But during the third quarter of 2006, 3700 Albertans moved to Saskatchewan—an increase of 1300 over the same period in 2005. The Saskatchewan government is encouraging the trend!

EARLY TRANSPORT

From the cart train to the B-train, Saskatchewan's modes of transport have come a long way in a short time. Check out the many ways to get from La Loche to Carnduff, from Lloydminster to Cumberland House, from Consul to…well, you get the idea!

Do-It-Yourself Travois

For generations, Native bands on the prairie travelled by foot, hauling supplies—and sometimes small children and elders—on travois. "Travois" were made of two long poles (lodgepole pine was the best) that were lashed together with wet rawhide at one end and spread apart at the other. A circular willow frame was fastened to the centre, then laced with rawhide straps. Dogs, and later horses, were harnessed to travois. Often two dogs were hitched together, their travois fastened together with a long crosspiece. An invalid could then lie across the "double travois," and the load was evenly distributed. Some travois trails (like the one near Clearwater Lake) are still visible on the landscape.

Horse Sense

Southern Native bands were the first to own horses. Fast horses that were used as buffalo runners were never hitched to travois. Young mothers with babies sometimes rode pack horses.

In a Rut

Before the railways arrived, the main method that settlers and surveyors used to haul freight across the prairie was the Red River cart—a two-wheeled wooden contraption pulled by an ox. Long lines of cart trains followed routes between fur-trading posts and settlements, often leaving a track that was 16 ruts wide, because it was easier for an ox to step into the wheel rut of the cart ahead of it, rather than following its predecessor's hoofprints. Some of the deep ruts left by carts following the Battleford Trail north from Swift Current can still be seen.

Bone Trail

Prior to the 1800s, buffalo provided Native bands with many necessities of daily life, including food and shelter. Between 1800 and 1900, huge herds of buffalo were slaughtered by traders and European and American hunters. Buffalo bones were transported along the "Bone Trail" to the railway in Saskatoon, where they were sent east to be used for lampblack (a common paint and ink pigment) and fertilizer.

Paint Your Wagon

For farm work, a homesteader needed a wagon. Pulled by stubborn oxen or by a prize-winning team of Clydesdales, wagons ranged from the simple dray to the three-decker grain wagon. Sometimes the only respite from the sun out on the bald prairie was the shady spot beneath the wagon!

Sleigh Bells Ring

Winter transport included ox sleighs, high-built cutters and humble sleds. Old-timers swear that in extreme cold they sometimes had to stop to clear the ice off the horses' frozen eyelashes.

Very Mushy

Early settlers used dog sleds for winter hauling. Dog sledding is now a popular sport, and annual competitions are held in the province. A team of huskies can travel at about 20 kilometres per hour.

Prairie Yacht Club

A Saskatchewan staple, the stoneboat is a rudimentary wooden raft used for rock-picking. In homesteading days, more than one desperate housewife was known to hitch an ox to the stoneboat in order drag herself over for a visit with the nearest neighbour.

TRAINS

I Hear that Train A-Comin'

Virtually every community in the province owes its existence to the railway. Between 1870 and 1914, the network of railway lines expanded quickly in order to move grain to domestic and foreign markets. Until the '30s, major communities had several trains a day heading out in every direction. At the railway system's peak in 1972, Saskatchewan had 14,560 kilometres of rail lines. The current provincial system is the largest of the three western provinces and has over 10,000 kilometres of rail, including 6500 kilometres of branch lines.

Flat Broke

Rumour has it that Sir John A. Macdonald ran out of money as he pushed the Canadian Pacific Railway (CPR) through Saskatchewan. Manitoba speculators were buying up railway right-of-way land at low prices then selling to the CPR as construction reached their property. To fool speculators, the CPR announced that it would build through the Qu'Appelle Valley, with Lumsden as the main terminal. After the speculators had used all their credit to buy land in the valley, the CPR built through the flatlands, making Regina the hotspot.

DID YOU KNOW?

The stretch of railway line between Regina and Stoughton runs 140 kilometres, without a bend, making it the longest straight line of rail in the world!

Steamed Up

The Western Development Museum in Moose Jaw operates the Short Line, a working steam train that runs on summer weekends.

AUTOMOBILES AND ROADS

Adopt-a-Highway

Early road-building in the province was labour intensive. In the north, teams of oxen had to be used to clear the brush. And for many years each settler was required to maintain any roads adjacent to his property!

Sticky Situation

Once automobiles appeared on the scene, Saskatchewan roads were found to be sadly lacking. Every time it rained, stuck vehicles would litter the roads. As late as 1926, the Trans-Canada Highway through Saskatchewan was only a dirt road.

DID YOU  KNOW?

Saskatchewan was the first province to complete its section of the Trans-Canada Highway. The 653-kilometre stretch was under construction from 1950 to 1957.

Around the World and Back Again... and Again...and Again...

On a per-capita basis, Saskatchewan has twice as many roads and highways as any other province in Canada. Saskatchewan's provincial and rural municipality road network could circle the equator 4.5 times!

Optimists

The post office north of Tisdale was named "Autoroad" in 1910—when there were no automobiles and very few roads in the area!

On the Road Again

Fifty-one percent of Saskatchewan's highway network is paved. The primary highways are numbered 1 through 40 and have speed limits ranging from 90 to 110 kilometres per hour.

The Naked Truth

What with recent railway branch line abandonment, many more big trucks are barrelling down Saskatchewan highways. As a protest against the condition of Highway #32 between Swift Current and the village of Leader, some of Leader's prominent residents posed naked, in potholes, for a 2007 calendar. One pothole was so large that a Leaderite was able to pose in it while sitting in his canoe—with the paddle strategically placed, of course!

That's Correct!

In the late 1800s, surveyors carved the Prairies into quarter sections that could be settled by immigrants. A quarter-section measured one-half mile by one-half mile (almost one kilometre by one kilometre) and contained 160 acres. A full section was one mile by one mile (1.5 kilometres by 1.5 kilometres), with 640 acres. Thirty-six sections made up a township, measuring six miles by six miles (9.5 kilometres by 9.5 kilometres). However, because these measurements were based on meridians, and because meridians become closer together as they run north, some adjustments were needed to keep the townships and sections equal in area. Slight "S" turns in the North-South roads correct for the curvature of the earth. These are called "correction lines."

Let's Go Riding in the Car-Car

Joseph Frederick Spalding, a photographer from Fernie, BC, was an early motor tourist. In the fall of 1913, Spalding racked up 37,000 kilometres travelling to hundreds of locations throughout BC, Alberta and Saskatchewan. Gas and oil for the journey cost $900, and he went through two complete sets of tires.

Come Away with Me, Lucille

In 1917, five Moose Javians imported enough parts to build 25 luxury cars. Unfortunately, it turned out that the investors were the only customers interested in the city's answer to Mercedes-Benz, and sadly, Moose Jaw's fledgling auto industry collapsed.

Dry Humour

During the Depression, gasoline became too expensive for many farm families. Once-useful autos were hitched to horses or oxen and pulled as wagons. These bulky conveyances were nick-named "Bennett Buggies," after Prime Minister R.B. Bennett, widely perceived as unsympathetic to the plight of farmers.

Take Off, Eh!

The word "hoser" originated in Saskatchewan, where it referred derisively to a person low enough to steal gasoline by siphoning it with a hose from someone else's tank.

Licence to Thrill

Saskatchewan licence plates currently boast a picture of three stalks of wheat and the slogan, "Land of Living Skies." There are more than 750,000 licensed vehicles and 115,000 licensed trailers in the province.

Purple Haze

For years, purple dye was added to gas used for off-road vehicles—it was cheaper because the road tax hadn't been paid on it. Farmers were allowed to use purple gas for their farm equipment only, but of course it was tempting to just fill up the car, too…. The dye remained in the vehicle's intake system for a long time so it was easy for police to find evidence. At one time, tickets for "getting caught with purple" were more common than tickets for drunk driving.

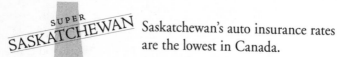 Saskatchewan's auto insurance rates are the lowest in Canada.

Get Horizontal

Saskatchewan is one of the few jurisdictions in North America (Alberta, New Mexico, Québec, Texas, Wisconsin, and the Yukon are the others) that mounts traffic lights with their faces arranged horizontally, often with vertical signals on the side.

Buckled Up

Saskatchewan leads the nation in obeying seat belt laws.

BOATS

Nautical History

From the 1870s to the 1890s, steamboats sailed the North Saskatchewan River. The swift current and shifting sandbars made navigation difficult, but the boats played an important role in transporting settlers and supplies. The steamboats were also a form of entertainment—the *Alberta* featured a cruise with a 20-piece orchestra on Saturday nights. As well, a steamboat named *Qu'Appelle* had ports of call on Last Mountain Lake.

Naval Battle

On May 9, 1885, during the Northwest Rebellion, General Middleton sent the paddle-wheeled steamboat the *Northcote* downriver in an attempt to take Batoche from the Métis. Gabriel Dumont quickly figured out that the steamer would have to pass through a rapid caused by a bend in the river, so the Métis strung an iron ferry cable across the water. The cable caught the funnel of the boat and started a fire. Some soldiers jumped overboard, the boat went adrift, and Saskatchewan's first and only naval battle was over!

Marine Disaster

The steamboat *The City of Medicine Hat* smashed into a pier of Saskatoon's Victoria Bridge on June 7, 1908. Cattle that were on the bridge above at the time promptly stampeded. All the crew, except the engineer who swam to shore, scrambled onto the bridge with the angry herd.

The Fleet

Saskatchewan's Department of Highways operates 12 ferries. The largest is the Riverhurst Ferry, which can accommodate 15 cars. In winter, ice roads are maintained at some ferry-crossing spots.

PLANES

Higher than a Kite

Bill Gibson, a hardware store owner, began experimenting with flying machines in 1904, just months after the Wright Brothers had made their first flight. Gibson was known as "The Balgonie Birdman" after he flew off the roof of his store in Balgonie.

DID YOU  KNOW?

In Saskatoon, the first airplane was owned by Bob St. Henry, who had it shipped via rail, in pieces. Its first flight was in May 1911.

Sky High

In 1912, a Curtiss pusher biplane named "The Shooting Star" was a big attraction at the Regina Exhibition.

Pioneer Pilot

The first commercial pilot in Canada was Regina's Roland Groome, who received his licence in April 1920. And the first licensed "air harbour" (airport) in Canada was Groome's airfield at the corner of Albert and McCallum in south Regina. Unfortunately, Groome was killed in a crash in 1935. Today, over 2500 Saskatchewanians have pilot's licences.

Chinese Air Force Base

In 1919, the Chinese National League established an air training school in Saskatoon. The Keng Wah Aviation school trained between 200 and 300 Chinese pilots for Sun Yat-sen's nationalist cause before the school closed its doors in the mid-1920s.

Aviatrix Tricks

Nellie Carson became the first woman in Saskatchewan to get her pilot's licence, in 1929. In 1931 she broke an altitude record by spiralling up to 4800 metres, without wearing an oxygen mask! "I damn near froze to death it was so cold," said Carson.

Another Feminine First

Joyce Bond was the first woman in western Canada to use a parachute when she made a 760-metre jump near Regina in 1937.

Air Ambulance First

Saskatchewan had the first provincial air ambulance service in North America and the Commonwealth, established by the province in 1946. Unofficial air ambulances had been operating in the province since the '30s. Pilots had patients' family members create special markers on the ground so that they'd be able to identify the locations—overalls were placed on the top of a windmill or a large circle of hay bales was made in the snow.

Here Come the High Flyers

In 1940, construction began on British Commonwealth Air Training Plan bases in 14 Saskatchewan communities. Thousands of young men from all over the Commonwealth poured into Saskatchewan, where they received a warm welcome.

Fighter Ace

The RCAF's top wartime fighter ace during World War II was Regina's Henry Wallace "Wally" McLeod, a former schoolteacher who served in Malta and northwestern Europe. He was killed in an aerial dogfight in September 1944.

Air Disaster

A Trans-Canada Airlines passenger plane collided with an RCAF trainer over Moose Jaw in 1954. Thirty-seven people died, and three houses were destroyed.

Smokejumpers

In the late 1940s, Saskatchewan created a unique team of aerial firefighters known as "Smokejumpers," who parachuted down into forest fires. The parachutes, 8.5 metres in diameter, landed with a jolt equivalent to stepping off a 3-metre fence, and the tools dropped down to the firefighters were basic: an axe-adze, shovels, saws and 22-litre canvas backpacks with a squirt hose. No other province or territory boasted an organization anything like the Smokejumpers. The unit was disbanded in the '60s, when helicopters became more available for firefighting.

Spread Your Shiny Wings and Fly Away

Canada's world-famous aerial acrobatic troupe, the Snowbirds, was formed at CFB Moose Jaw in 1971. The CT-114 Tutor jets reach speeds of almost 600 kilometres per hour, and sometimes fly in formation less than 1.5 metres apart. The Snowbirds crest depicts four "speedbirds" in a formation that resembles an ear of wheat—a tribute to their home province.

Heads Up!

Saskatchewan has 150 community-owned airports and airstrips, from those serving remote communities in the north to the two major airports in Saskatoon and Regina. One of the busiest airports in Canada is the one at 15 Wing Moose Jaw. On May 27, 1977, the 15 Wing ATC Squadron controlled 3301 aircraft takeoffs and landings in a 24-hour period, setting an all-time North American record.

Exotic Ports of Call

Steve Fossett, one of the world's greatest adventurers, has set 115 new world records or world "firsts," one of which was "First Solo Flight Across the Pacific, Absolute World Distance." Fossett logged 8740 kilometres in February 1995—flying from Seoul, South Korea, to Mendam, Saskatchewan.

BRIDGES

Bridge Over Every Sort of Water

Bridges of all shapes and sizes abound in the province. Saskatoon is known as the "City of Bridges"—by 1908 three railway bridges and a traffic bridge crossed the South Saskatchewan River. Today, the city has seven bridges. Other notable Saskatchewan bridges include the McCloy Creek CNR train trestle west of Melfort, a massive wooden bridge built in 1929 that's been declared a Heritage Site, and the beautiful 457-metre-long railway bridge west of Watrous.

Walk This Way

The SkyTrail Bridge in Outlook is the longest pedestrian bridge in Canada. It runs for 914 metres over the South Saskatchewan River, at a height of over 45 metres.

SUPER SASKATCHEWAN Wolseley has a 103-metre "swinging bridge" over Fairly Lake.

The Long and the Short of It

And Regina has the Albert Street Bridge, which is the largest bridge over the shortest span of water in the world!

OTHER TRANSPORTATION

Up, Up, and Away

In the summer of 1908, hot-air balloons delighted audiences at fairs and exhibitions across the province.

I Don't Want a Pickle

Motorcycle enthusiasts in Saskatchewan have often been innovators. In 1917, Reverend Melly adapted the wheels of his motorbike so that he could ride it on railway tracks. More recently, Ed Medici and his daughter Holly came up with a "female-friendly," gearless, chainless, shiftless motorcycle that eliminates 85 percent of all moving parts!

Snow Plane

In 1929, at the age of 19, Spy Hill native Karl Lorch designed, built and patented the first propeller-driven snowplane. The motorized sleds helped conquer isolation in rural Canada until the advent of all-weather roads in the 1950s.

Snow Job

Before snowmobiles were commercially available, some ingenious farmers designed their own. Here's how Eddy Stockman of the Beechy area built a snowmobile, circa 1948:

- ☛ Boil the ends of some 12' (3.5-metre) wooden boards and fashion them into a curve. Make steering skis the same way. Let them dry all summer.

- ☛ After harvest, assemble the curved boards with crosspieces to make a toboggan 12' (3.5 metres) long and 3' (one metre) wide.

- ☛ Order a 15 horse power Indian motorcycle engine from Princess Auto in Winnipeg.

- ☛ Build a track 6' (1.5 metres) long and 12' (3.5 metres) wide. Use the sprockets and chains from a feeder chain from an old combine. Manufacture the cleats yourself.

- ☛ Cut a 14' wide (35 centimetre) slot in the rear and centre of the toboggan, and install the track. Mount the engine in front.

- ☛ Hook up the track so that it's driven by the transmission and the drive shaft, using a #60 roller chain to complete the drive train.

- ☛ Install the steering skis and link them to a steering gearbox and a steering wheel from an old car.

- ☛ Attach fuel tank and ignition.

- ☛ Paint it red.

- ☛ Drive it into town.

Eddy's snow machine ran very well, and he used it until he and his wife moved to town. Eventually, Bombardier began mass-marketing Ski-Doos, and the rest is history. Saskatchewan has 10,000 kilometres of groomed snowmobile trails today.

Clang, Clang, Clang

At one time, Saskatoon, Moose Jaw and Regina all had streetcar systems. A 1949 fire in Regina destroyed half of the city's running stock. When the trams were retired, old cars often turned up as roadside lunch counters.

The Bus Project

In 2005, a group of Regina artists decided to create art in an unusual venue—in buses and bus terminals! "The Bus Project" explored bus travel and the immigrant experience and included video art in Saskatchewan Transportation Company terminals and fabric artistry on bus seat covers.

Shank's Mare

Until 1986, Saskatoon featured nine crosswalks called "Scramble Corners." Not only could you cross the street the usual way, but traffic was halted in both directions so that a pedestrian could choose to walk diagonally across the entire intersection. This was sometimes a challenge to do in the allotted time: At the Scramble Corner on 2nd Avenue and 23rd street, a sign that read "Wait for the signal to walk" was changed by a wag who had crossed out "walk" and substituted the word "run."

ExpressPost

In the early days, mail made its way to settlers by any means available. Trains, dog sleds, horses, wagons, sleighs, steamboats and paddle boats all played a part. NWMP members delivered a lot of letters, and often a homesteader would simply be entrusted to deliver mail to his neighbours.

ROADSIDE ATTRACTIONS

It's a province full of surprises. Swim in Saskatchewan's salty inland sea…Explore Al Capone's rum-running tunnels…and hey, look at all that big stuff at the side of the road!

Big Stuff

Many of the province's roadside attractions make perfect sense: White Bear has a polar bear, Indian Head has an Indian head, Moose Jaw has a moose…you get the idea. But you may have to do a bit of travelling to find out the stories behind some of Saskatchewan's big stuff:

Allan	Combine in the Sky
Aylesbury	Ox and Cart; Wire Buffalo
Bellevue	Pea Plant
Biggar	Hanson Buck
Borden	Buffalo
Cabri*	Antelope and Wheat
Canora	Lesia the Ukrainian Girl
Chamberlain	Lilies
Chaplin	Avocet; Piping Plover
Churchbridge	Loonie
Coronach	Race Horse
Craik	Buffalo Hunter
Craven	Guitar
Cut Knife	Tomahawk; Guitar
Daphne	Tire People
Davidson	Coffee Pot and Cup
Dundurn	Bone Gatherer; Horse and Wagon

Edam	Windmill
Englefeld	Pig
Esterhazy	Pete the Miner; Potash Borer; Sheave Wheel
Estevan	Lignite Louis
Eston	Gopher
Fort Qu'Appelle	Tipi
Girvin	Buffalo and Cart
Goodsoil	Gus the Lumberjack
Gorlitz	Antlers
Govan	Walter the Whooping Crane
Gronlid	Globe
Hanley	Opera House; Cairn
Herschel	Grizzly Bear
Hudson Bay	Lumberjack; Millennium Moose

Humboldt	Diefenbaker Stamp
Indian Head	Indian Head
Kelvington	Hockey Cards
Kenaston	Snowman
Kerrobert	Canada Goose Water Tower
Kindersley	Canada Goose
Kyle	Wally the Wooly Mammoth
Lancer	Chokecherry
Langenburg	World's Highest Swing
Lashburn	Barr Colonists Memorial
Leader	Burrowing Owls; Mule Deer; Kangaroo Rats; Red-Headed Woodpecker; Sturgeon; Meadowlark; Rattlesnake; Cactus; Hawk
Lloydminster	Border Markers
Macklin	Bunnock
Maidstone	Canola Plant
Melville	Buffalo; Lilies
Moose Jaw	Mac the Moose; Sukanen Ship
Morse	Cattails
North Battleford	Buffalo; RCMP; Giant Ice Cube Melt
Ogema	Indian Head; Ralph the Grasshopper
Outlook	Rainbow
Paradise Hill	Ox and Cart
Parkside	Lilies
Pierceland	Butterfly
Ponteix	Mo the Dinosaur
Porcupine Plain	Quilly Willy the Porcupine
Prince Albert	Tire Man; Wheat Stalks

Quill Lake	Canada Goose
Radisson	Red Bull
Redvers	NWMP
Regina	Pemmican Pete; Pitchfork; Polar Bear; Reginald the Grasshopper
Riverhurst	Northern Pike
Rocanville	Baseball Cap; Diamond; Oil Can
Rosthern	Wheat Sheaf
Sceptre	Wheat Stalks
Sheho	Sharp-Tailed Grouse
Spiritwood	Wolf
Spy Hill	Snow Plane
Sturgis	Cowboy and Horse
St. Walburg	Chuckwagon Racer
Swift Current	Buffalo
Tantallon	White-Tailed Deer
Tisdale	Honeybee
Turtleford	Ernie the Turtle
Vonda	Still
Watson	Santa Claus
Weyburn	Lighthouse Water Tower; Prairie Lily; Wheat Sculptures
White Bear	Polar Bear
White Fox	White Fox
Wilkie	Grasshopper
Willow Bunch	Willow Bunch Giant
Yorkton	Missile

*Ralph Berg of Cabri makes a lot of the big stuff you see at the sides of Canadian roads!

PLACE NAMES

Mixed Messages

Eastend is in the western part of Saskatchewan; North Portal is on the southern boundary; West End is in the east; and Southend is in the north.

Physically Fit

It's possible to tour Saskatchewan body part by body part: Indian Head, Moose Jaw, Eyebrow, Eye Hill Rural Municipality, Elbow, Arm River, Knee Lake, Bone Creek...

No, Dildo Is in Newfoundland

Saskatchewan has towns named "Climax" and "Love." Apparently it's tough Love, though—events at the annual Love's Valentine Winter Festival include sawing, nail driving, hatchet throwing, pillow fighting, arm wrestling and a power saw competition.

Boning Up

The original name of Regina was "Pile o' Bones," a corruption
of the Cree "oscana ka-asasteki," or "where the bones are piled."
The site of the settlement had been a popular buffalo hunting
spot, and Natives heaped buffalo bones together, believing that
the animals would stay close to a spot containing the remains of
their fellows. Wascana Lake in Regina's city centre was named
with an approximation of the Cree word.

Run into Town on a Rail

Many communities in Saskatchewan were named by railway
employees. There were three general types of names:

☞ Names with local meaning; variations on Native words
or names that described the landscape

☞ Names of places from other countries (the Scots heritage
of railway bigshots is obvious!)

☞ Names of people—famous, infamous and obscure

Now I Know My ABCs

The Grand Trunk Pacific railway line's gimmick was to name
stations on its main line in alphabetical order, giving us Allan,
Bradwell, Clavet, Duro, Earl…all the way down the line to
Unity, Vera, Winter, Yonker and Zumbro.

Reading Railway

The Canadian National Railway, in contrast, peppered one of
its lines with literary luminaries of the day: Service, Cowper,
Carlyle, Wordsworth, Browning, Lampman and Hardy, among
others.

Cockeyed Optimists

A lot of town names reflected early settlers' hopes and optimism: Abound, Choiceland, Fortune, Goodsoil, Paradise Hill, Plenty, Success, Superb, Supreme…. In 1884, about 30 Jewish families established a colony they named "New Jerusalem." Unfortunately, their first two crops failed, and their rabbi got frostbite and had to have his feet amputated. A more successful Jewish settlement, Wapella, followed.

In February, who could resist a trip to Java, Kandahar, Key West, Valparaiso or Ceylon—all in Saskatchewan!

Calling River

The beautiful Qu'Appelle Valley was called "kah-tep-was," or "river that calls," by the Cree. Legend has it that a man on his way home to marry his sweetheart was paddling on the river when he heard his name being called. He thought he recognized his bride's voice, so answered, "Who calls?" but got no response. Again he heard his name, and again he asked, "Who calls?" The man arrived home a few days later to find his bride had died, calling his name with her last breath. "Qu'Appelle" means "who calls," in French.

Saskatoon Pie
In 1834 John Neilson Lake took on the task of finding the best townsite for a temperance colony in the Northwest Territories. After a lengthy and exhausting journey, he was resting in his tent near the banks of the South Saskatchewan River when a member of his party showed him a branch of berries. Lake jumped to his feet and shouted, "Arise, Saskatoon, Queen of the North!" The temperance colony was established as Saskatoon, on that spot.

The People Are Politer, Too

A sign outside Biggar reads, "New York Is Big, But This Is Biggar."

CITIES

The Stats

Type of Municipality	Number	Minimum Population Criteria
Cities	13	5000
Towns	145	500
Villages	289	100
Resort Villages	39	none
Rural Municipalities	296	none
Organized Hamlets	169	45 voters
Northern Hamlets	9	50
Northern Towns	2	500
Northern Villages	13	100

Borderline
Lloydminster is the only city in Canada located on a border. The main street runs along the fourth meridian, which is one of the longest, straight surveyed lines in the world.

City Highlights

First: Regina. Both Regina and Moose Jaw incorporated as cities in 1903, but Moose Jaw lost out by a few months.

Newest: Humboldt. Incorporated in 2000 as a city, Humboldt is the baby of the bunch.

Largest: Saskatoon. In the early 20th century, Moose Jaw had the largest population. Then Regina held the title. Now Saskatoon wins, with a population of 209,015.

Most Crowded: Regina. Not a problem anywhere in the province, really, but it has the densest population, with 1502 people every square kilometre.

Wealthiest: Estevan. Median income for citizens over the age of 15 is $25,400.

Oldest: Melville. Average age of a Melvillian is 44.9.

Youngest: Lloydminster. Average age of the people on the Saskatchewan side of Lloyd is 26.8.

Most Affordable Housing: Melville. An average home can be yours for $57,630.

Highest: Swift Current. At an altitude of 817 metres above sea level, "Speedy Creek" comes out on top.

Lowest: Prince Albert. The city wins the limbo contest, at 428 metres above sea level.

Coldest Winter: Prince Albert. Temperatures in January average -19°C.

Hottest Summer: Estevan. The median temp in July is a tropical 19.5°C.

Windiest: Swift Current. Average annual wind speed clocked in at 19.7 kilometres per hour.

Nicknames

City	Nickname
Estevan	Energy City
Humboldt	A Little Bit of Germany in the Heart of the Prairies
Lloydminster	Border City
Melfort	City of Northern Lights
Melville	The Rail Centre
Moose Jaw	The Friendly City
North Battleford	Oasis on the Prairies
Prince Albert	Gateway to the North
Regina	Queen City
Saskatoon	City of Bridges
Swift Current	Hub of the Great Southwest
Weyburn	The Hospitality Capital
Yorkton	Where Good Things Happen

POINTS OF INTEREST

Top Ten List

Two of Saskatchewan's lakes are on the list of the 10 largest freshwater lakes in North America. Lake Athabasca (7935 square kilometres) is number 9, and Reindeer Lake (6650 square kilometres) is number 10.

Lest We Forget

All Saskatchewan armed forces personnel who died during World War II have been honoured with a lake named after them, thanks to the Saskatchewan Geo-Memorial Project, which began in 1947.

Older Than the Pyramids

Wanuskewin Heritage Park north of Saskatoon offers a glimpse at a civilization more than 6000 years old. Nomadic tribes gathered to hunt bison, gather food and herbs and seek shelter from winter winds. Archeologists have found tipi rings, a medicine wheel, pottery fragments and other artifacts of ancient life.

Have You Seen Marie Antoinette?

During the Battle of Batoche in 1885, the bell at the mission was taken as a war trophy by a member of the North West Field Force. The bell—which had been blessed and given the name "Marie Antoinette" to honour the Virgin Mary and St. Anthony of Padua—was eventually found in a Legion hall in Millbrook, Ontario. Negotiations were underway to return it to its home in Batoche when it was stolen. To the Métis Nation, the bell has become a symbol of the many things lost at Batoche in 1885.

Healing Waters

Little Manitou Lake near Watrous is saltier than the Dead Sea; it has a specific gravity of 1.06, which means you can't help but float like a cork in the water! Brine shrimp—a.k.a "Sea Monkeys"—are plentiful in the salty brew.

Danceland

Next to Manitou Beach is world-famous Danceland. The hall's maple-wood dance floor rests on a 15–25 centimetre cushion of horsehair, allowing dancers to glide across it with ease. In the 1920s, "jitney dances" were held at Danceland—men bought tickets for 10¢ each (or three for a quarter) and exchanged them for a turn on the dance floor. Every night 500 people came to trip the light fantastic, and some of the best bands in the country performed there, including Wilf Carter, Don Messer, the Inkspots, and Gene Dloughy.

Call of the Wild

Saskatchewan has 34 provincial parks, covering over one million square hectares. Cypress Hills Interprovincial Park straddles the Saskatchewan-Alberta border. Clearwater River, Athabasca Sand Dunes, Wildcat Hill, and Clarence-Steepbank Lakes have been designated as wilderness parks.

Bring Your Trunks
Lac La Ronge Provincial Park has more water than land! It contains more than 100 lakes.

Park It

Saskatchewan has two national parks: Prince Albert National Park and Grasslands National Park, and over 100 regional parks.

Watching All the Birds Go By
In 2001, the United Nations designated the Redberry Pelican project a world biosphere reserve. Redberry Lake, a saline lake near Hafford, is the summer nesting ground of the white pelican and many other bird species. The lake is one of only thirteen biospheres designated in Canada.

But Don't Get Goosed by the Geese
Wascana Park in Regina covers 1100 hectares, making it one of the largest urban parks in the world.

Sands of Time

In the north, the constantly moving Athabasca Sand Dunes reach a height of 30 metres and stretch 100 kilometres along the shore of Lake Athabasca. The dunes are home to 10 plant species found nowhere else in the world. The Great Sand Hills west of Swift Current make up the largest uninterrupted area of sand dunes in southern Canada. They cover an area of 1911 square kilometres.

Early Bulletin Board

Near the village of Roche Percee (French for "pierced rock")
is the gigantic landmark that gave the community its name:
a sandstone rock pierced by holes. Early travellers used the rock
as a guidepost, and General Custer and the men of the ill-fated
Seventh Cavalry stopped to write their names on it. When the
wind blows, the rock makes spooky music.

Treed

The biggest tree in Saskatchewan is just outside Blaine Lake.
With a diameter of 1.5 metres, the tree is estimated to be well
over 100 years old.

Saskatchewan's oldest existing building is the Holy Trinity Anglican Church at Stanley Mission, built between 1854 and 1860. Ten thousand pieces of stained glass for the windows were shipped from England.

For Whom the Bell Tolls

In 1881, Major W.R. Bell bought 53,000 acres of land just north of Indian Head. A massive 16-room stone house and a beautiful, round stone barn went up the following year. Two hundred horses and 73 plows were used during the breaking of the virgin prairie. The venture teetered on the brink of bankruptcy for several years until a fire in 1893 and a crop failure the following year put an end to it.

Horseshoe's Barn

In 1915, William "Horseshoe" Smith built a barn west of Leader that measured 120 metres long and 40 metres wide. The barn was so big that at the grand opening, two bands were hired— one to play at each end! Today, only the foundation is left of what was thought to have been North America's largest barn.

Shattered

A 400-ton rock that once served as a ceremonial place for Natives was destroyed in 1966 during construction of the Gardiner Dam. Nicknamed "Mistaseni," the giant glacial remnant from the Canadian Shield had been a favourite place for buffalo to rub their matted coats. Natives placed offerings to Manitou at the rock's base, and later, white settlers in the area came to picnic in its shade. A movement to relocate Mistaseni was launched, but the rock was just too large and heavy. Instead, fragments of it were placed in a cairn near the Elbow Harbour.

Dam Site

And the Gardiner Dam itself was the world's largest earth-filled dam when it opened in 1967. The project took eight years to complete and used 65 million cubic metres of dirt. The dam is 5 kilometres long and 64 metres high, and the spillway can discharge 7500 cubic metres of water per second. The dam provides irrigated water to 106,210 acres of farmland, as well as drinking water for half the province, including the cities of Regina, Saskatoon and Moose Jaw.

Soddie

Several locations in Saskatchewan, including the museum in Elbow, feature a sod house patterned after those of the early settlers. Homesteaders lifted strips of sod and cut them into rectangles (usually one-metre slabs). These were piled up to create walls, leaving spaces for small windows and a door. Floors were dirt, and roofs were sometimes frame constructs that were thatched or covered with sod. These "soddies" were warm in winter and cool in summer, but as the saying goes, "When it rained outside for a day, it rained inside for three days." Bugs and other critters emerging from the kitchen walls were a challenge for pioneer women, too.

Gentleman's Paradise

In 1882, Captain Edward Pierce established the community of Cannington Manor in the southeast corner of the province. His intention was to build a society of Victorian gentlemen farmers. By the mid-1890s more than 200 people lived at Cannington Manor, including the Beckton brothers of Manchester—who built "Didsbury," a 26-room, two-storey mansion complete with bay windows, a large verandah, an Italian marble staircase, Turkish carpets and gilt-framed paintings. Didsbury was one of the largest houses in Canada at the time, and cost over

$3 million then. The Becktons' 2600-acre estate included an 18-man fieldstone bunkhouse, kennels for foxhounds and stone stables with mahogany stalls.

While nearby settlers in soddies and shacks eked out a living, the gentlemen of Cannington Manor attended plays, took sketching lessons from noted British artists, played billiards or went foxhunting in boots, breeches and hunting coats. A billiards room at Didsbury featured valets who served drinks, ironed newspapers and cleaned guns for the guests. Alfred Lord Tennyson's nephew played for the community's rugby team, the Cannington Combines. Many of the inhabitants of the settlement were "remittance men"—men sent abroad by their families due to transgressions in England, living on money sent from home. Very little farming was done, but quite a lot of drinking was. When Pierce died, the colony was left leaderless and it eventually disintegrated.

In-tents

The world's largest inhabited tipi is the facility that houses the Treaty Four Governance Centre in Fort Qu'Appelle. It has a diameter of 213 metres and is 33 metres tall.

Check Me in Right Now

Temple Gardens Mineral Spa in Moose Jaw is a 4.5 star resort hotel that has a large, naturally warm indoor and outdoor mineral pool. The waters for the pools are drawn from ancient seabeds that are more than one kilometre below the surface.

Shiver Me Timbers

On the top of Pirot Hill on the shores of Jackfish Lake is a lighthouse! Built as a tourist attraction, the lighthouse is 11 metres tall, and the beacon can be seen for several kilometres.

Rootbound

Canada's largest genealogical lending library is in Regina. The Saskatchewan Genealogical Society has over 20,000 items to help you locate branches of your family tree.

The Great Wall of Smiley

In 1962, Albert Johnson was picking rocks on his farm near Smiley. For a lark, he started arranging the stones in the shape of a wall. After 29 years of adding rocks, he built a wall that is now more than half a kilometre long with an average height of 1.5 metres. It was constructed without cement or mortar and is as high as 3.5 metres in some places.

Funomenal

Buena Vista resident Gerri Ann Siwek and her husband Steve Karch run what may be the world's smallest museum: the Funomena Mobile Museum of the Weird and Strange. With 13 exhibits and its own souvenir shop, Funomena is housed in a trailer and travels the plains. Exhibits include psychic frogs, a portrait of Elvis with real Elvis hair, Satan's fork, and the live half-fish, half-human.

EVENTS

Meet Me at the Fair

The Great Territorial Fair took place in Regina in 1895. On exhibit were 900 head of cattle, along with local products such as buggies, buffalo coats, saddles and beer. Entertainment included a snake charmer, a trick bicyclist, and Moosewa, a Native sprinter from Alberta who took on all challengers.

A Really Big Show

In 1971, Regina established Canadian Western Agribition. It's now known as North America's second-largest annual livestock show, with over 4000 head of livestock on display over six days. Agribition also hosts 450 trade show exhibits.

Perogies to Die For

The Vesna Festival in Saskatoon—with traditional dancing, music and displays—is billed as the "World's Largest Ukrainian Cabaret."

How Much Is that Sundoggy in the Window?

The Sundog Handcraft Faire in Saskatoon is the largest event of its kind in western Canada. Artists and artisans converge to display handmade jewellery, knitted items, candles, leatherwork, birchbark crafts, toys…and much more. Specialty food producers sell fudge, pepper jellies, gourmet popcorn, along with many saskatoon berry–filled items.

Royalty

Several northern communities hold "King and Queen Trapper" competitions. One of the liveliest is held annually in La Ronge, where contestants have to demonstrate their skills in jigging, moose calling, trap setting, leg wrestling, traditional portage, ice chiselling, tea boiling, bannock-making, traditional snow-shoeing, log tossing, log sawing, log splitting, nail driving and axe throwing.

Smokin'!

The highlight of the annual Gronlid Sports Day is the "Smoke Show." The idea is for contestants to fry their tires! A street in Gronlid is blocked off and lined with fencing and barrels. Drivers "give 'er" until something blows up—tires, transmissions, engines, whatever. Look out for those flying chunks of rubber!

Splat

The village of Cupar drops stuffed gopher facsimiles and foam gopher holes out of a hot-air balloon in order to raise money for their community. Residents sell tickets on the numbered gophers, and when the gophers land on the ground, they are checked to see which gopher landed closest to which numbered gopher hole. The winning gophers are then matched with prizes, and lucky winners take home the loot. The fundraiser has made well over $100,000.

Gopher Broke!

Every July, Eston holds its "Gopher Derby." Eight gophers at a time race—each in its own personal track—to a "finish hole" at the end. Pari-mutual betting with a tote board lets spectators put their money on the rodents that look most likely to win, place or show.

Rub-A-Dub-Dubbie

The town of Lumsden holds an annual "Duck Derby." Numbered rubber duckies are dumped into the Lumsden Creek and "race" for the finish-line one kilometre downstream.

Do You Hear Thunder?

During the 1930s, the village of St. Boswells held annual farting contests. The criteria for victory were length and volume—and the perennial winner's secret was rumoured to be a steady diet of sauerkraut and pigs' feet! A local merchant who had a general store close to the contest site was nervous about the flammability of methane. He always posted "No Smoking" signs in the area—making him way ahead of the curve on Saskatchewan's no-smoking legislation.

Sore Winner

In Beechy in the 1940s, the annual St. Patrick's Day dance inspired a "Homely Man's Contest," with the winner receiving a prize of a new pipe and a pouch of tobacco. Year after year the same man took the title—until one year the judges decided to award it to someone else. Both the winner and the loser that year were furious: the winner because he felt he was totally undeserving of the honour, and the loser because he'd been counting on getting the pipe and tobacco!

PEOPLE WHO MADE A DIFFERENCE

Ordinary people astonish us with extraordinary acts. Through the years, Saskatchewan has been home to more than its fair share of courageous citizens. And although it's hard to find official statistics on the subject, people in the know suspect that Saskatchewan also houses a large percentage of the country's most colourful characters...

The Honour Roll

Sixteen men associated with Saskatchewan have won the Victoria Cross, the highest recognition of valour in the British Commonwealth:

☞ Sergeant A.H.L. Richardson, 1900

☞ Corporal Harry Churchill Beet, 1901

☞ Lieutenant Hampden Cockburn, 1901

☞ Lieutenant Corporal Michael O'Leary, 1915

☞ Lieutenant Robert Combe, 1917

☞ Private William Milne, 1917

☞ Sergeant Harry Mullin, 1917

☞ Major George Randolph Pearkes, 1917

☞ Sergeant Hugh Cairns, 1918

☞ Lieutenant Edmund De Wind, 1918

☞ Lieutenant Gordon Flowerdew, 1918

☞ Sergeant Arthur Knight, 1918

☞ Sergeant Raphael Zengel, 1918

☞ Sergeant Major John Osborne, 1941

☞ Lieutenant Colonel Charles Merritt, 1942

☞ Major David Currie, 1944

Valour

Sergeant Hugh Cairns also received France's highest tribute, the Legion of Honour. Here's a summary of what Cairns did on one incredible day in November 1918:

☞ He single-handedly rushed a machine-gun post that fired on his platoon, killed five men and captured the gun.

☞ Cairns then repeated his one-man assault on a second machine-gun nest, killing 12 enemy soldiers and capturing 18.

☞ Next, he led a small party of men to outflank enemy artillery. Many Germans were killed, and about 50 surrendered.

☞ Finally, he went with a battle patrol and forced 60 enemy soldiers to surrender. While disarming these men, Cairns was severely wounded. Despite the injury, he opened fire and inflicted heavy losses before collapsing. He died the following day.

Streets in both Saskatoon and Valenciennes, France, are named for Cairns. In Saskatoon, a school, a baseball field and the armoury building also bear his name.

Hero of the Normandy Campaign

Major David Currie received the only Victoria Cross awarded to a Canadian soldier during the Normandy campaign from June to August 1944. On August 18, Currie went alone on foot into the German-held village of St. Lambert-sur-Dives to rescue crews of two disabled tanks under his command. The following morning, Currie's 115 men attacked the village—which was occupied by 3000 enemy soldiers. The Canadians destroyed seven tanks, twelve 88-mm guns, and killed or captured hundreds of Germans. The village was taken for the Allies, thus cutting off one of the Nazis' main escape routes. After his military career, Currie was the Sergeant-at-Arms in the House of Commons. The armoury in Moose Jaw is named after him.

World War I

Of the 42,000 Saskatchewan men and women who served in World War I, 4400 were killed. George Lawrence Price of Moose Jaw was the last soldier killed in the war. He died at Mons, Belgium, about two minutes before the armistice was signed on November 11, 1918.

World War II and Korea

Over 70,000 Saskatchewanians enlisted during World War II, and 3880 were killed. About 1000 people from Saskatchewan also served in the Korean War, and 29 died there.

Shady Story

Gerald Bertrand grew up in Radville, a dusty prairie town. In 1936, at the height of the Dust Bowl, Jerry was 16 and had an impossible dream: He wanted a hometown filled with trees. After raising money with various projects, in 1938 Bertrand led a crew that planted 2800 trees in the town and then hauled water to keep them alive. A few years later, Bertrand enlisted in the army, and he died overseas. But because of his efforts, Radville is now graced with tall, leafy trees.

Big Brass

One of Canada's best-known military leaders, General A.G.L. McNaughton, was born in Moosomin in 1887. A brigadier commanding artillery by the end of World War I, McNaughton returned to the army to command Canadian Forces at the outbreak of World War II. He eventually became defense minister and a Canadian delegate to the United Nations.

Better Late Than Never

In March 2007, 87-year-old Saskatchewan soldier Matt Gress was given France's highest military award—the Medal of the Knight of the Legion of Honour—for a battle that nearly killed him in 1944. Mr. Gress said he accepted the award in memory of fellow soldiers who did not survive.

Here's Looking at You, Kid

Sergeant Bill, a goat from Broadview, went to World War I as the mascot of the Fifth Canadian Infantry Battalion. Bill was gassed at Ypres and got a shrapnel wound at Festhubert. On his return to Canada, he received the 1914 Star, the General Service Medal, and the Victory Medal! Sergeant Bill (now stuffed) can be seen in the Broadview Museum.

ADVENTURERS AND ACHIEVERS

Lone Canadian Voice

Gladys Arnold, born in Macoun, Saskatchewan, went to work as a journalist at the *Regina Leader-Post* during the Depression. In 1935, disillusioned by capitalism's failure to deal with the unemployment crisis in North America, Arnold travelled to Germany to check out Hitler's employment program. Arnold was very quickly disgusted by fascism and spent the next few years trying to warn Canadians about the impending war. At the outbreak of World War II, Arnold was the only Canadian correspondent in Europe. She escaped Paris hours before the Nazis marched in, and she stayed in Europe to help the French resistance. In 1971, France named her a Chevalier of the Legion of Honour. Gladys Arnold died in 2002 at the age of 97.

Tall Tale

Edouard Beaupre was the first of 20 children born to average-sized parents near the village of Willowbunch in the late 19th century. Edouard grew at a normal rate for the first few years of his life, but by the time he was nine years old, he was 6 feet (almost 2 metres) tall. Beaupre dreamed of being a cowboy, but by his teens he was so tall that his feet dragged on the ground when he straddled a horse. He eventually reached a height of 8 feet, 2 inches (2.5 metres), and weighed slightly less than 400 pounds (182 kilograms). Trying to find a way to make money for his family, Beaupre joined a freak show and began touring North America; he died while performing with the Barnum & Bailey Circus at the 1904 World's Fair in St. Louis. The "Willowbunch Giant" was only 23 years old.

Beaupre's life story is sad enough—but further indignities followed. When Gaspard Beaupre tried to claim his son's body, he was told that doctors in St. Louis had the legal right to keep the corpse for research purposes. However, Edouard's former agent was able to retrieve the body and had it embalmed—he then put it on display and charged admission. Soon the giant's body was back on the freak-show circuit. When the circus went bankrupt, the corpse was stored in a warehouse. In the 1970s, relatives learned that Edouard's nude body had ended up in a glass case at the University of Montréal, and they tried to reclaim it. After years of delay, the university at last agreed to release Beaupre's remains. In a family ceremony in 1990, his ashes were buried close to the statue of him that stands in front of the Willowbunch Museum.

Friendly Neighbourhood Spiderman

Amateur arachnophile Donald J. Buckle of Preeceville has had two spiders named after him: *Ebo bucklei* and *Pardosa bucklei*.

Poundmaker

Poundmaker, a Cree leader, refused at first to sign Treaty 6, lobbying hard for a provision that would guarantee his people food in time of famine. With the buffalo gone, Natives on the prairies were facing starvation. When the Northwest Rebellion began in 1885, Poundmaker sent a message to the Indian agent in Battleford, saying he and his band of 60 were coming to ask for food rations. But the residents of Battleford were terrified of an attack and holed themselves up in the fort. Poundmaker's hungry people looted the houses. In retaliation, the militia headed for Poundmaker's camp at Cut Knife Creek. The Natives counterattacked, and Lieutenant Colonel William Otter's 500 men had to retreat. Some of the Natives wanted to give chase, but Poundmaker convinced them to let the soldiers go. Although he probably prevented a slaughter, Poundmaker was sentenced to three years in Stoney Mountain Penitentiary.

Big Bear

Big Bear (Mistahimusqua), chief of a mixed Cree and Ojibwa band, also refused to sign Treaty 6 and was convinced that overt resistance to the white man was doomed to failure. The increasing desperation of his band members caused them to question Big Bear's authority, and in 1885 more aggressive members of the band resorted to violence, killing nine white settlers at Frog Lake and burning Fort Pitt. Big Bear was convicted of treason and was also sent to Stoney Mountain. He was released two years later but was broken in spirit and died shortly afterwards.

Treehugger

Richard St. Barbe Baker is credited with the planting and protection of 11 billion trees. "St. Barbe," as he was known, was so disturbed by the relentless ploughing and wasteful logging practices he observed when he lived in Saskatchewan as a young man that he became a crusader for the ecology. St. Barbe's work as a conservationist took him around the world, but he is buried at the fittingly named Woodlawn Cemetery in Saskatoon.

Amazing Feets

Alvin Law was born in Yorkton in the early 1960s. His mother had taken the anti-morning sickness drug Thalidomide during her pregnancy, and Alvin was born without arms. When his parents gave him up for adoption, Alvin was sent to a foster home. Foster parents Hilda and Jack Law soon had Alvin holding his bottle, then learning to feed himself, dress himself and comb his hair—all with this feet. Soon Hilda even had Alvin using his toes to thread needles and sew on buttons!

The Laws insisted Alvin do chores like other children—mowing the lawn and washing dishes. Later he learned to bowl and to drive an unmodified car. In high school Alvin took up drums, piano and trombone and so excelled at the trombone that he was invited to play with the All-Star Band at the Canadian Stage Band Finals. He also took a shot at a seat in the Saskatchewan Legislature and once played a major role in an episode of *The X-Files*. Alvin is married, a father, and works as a motivational speaker.

Four from the Fourth Estate

Some of Canada's favourite journalists came from Saskatchewan:

☛ Pamela Wallin hosted *Canada AM, Pamela Wallin Live,* and the Canadian edition of *Who Wants To Be a Millionaire.* Prime Minister Jean Chretien appointed her Canada's Consul General in New York City in 2002. Wallin is from Wadena, where the main street is now named "Pamela Wallin Drive."

☛ Earl Cameron of Moose Jaw was CBC-TV's national news anchor during the 1960s. He also hosted the opinion show *Viewpoint* and is known to those of us of a certain age as the man who provided the voice-over for the Crest toothpaste "Look Ma, No Cavities" commercials.

☛ Allan Fotheringham, Canada's most famous political columnist, was born in Herne, Saskatchewan, in 1934. The back page of *Maclean's* often belongs to "Dr. Foth."

☛ Keith Morrison, correspondent for NBC's *Dateline* program, was born in Lloydminster and graduated from the University of Saskatchewan. He's also the stepfather of *Friends* actor Matthew Perry.

CHARACTERS

But Did It Match that Pointy Hat?

Harry Daniels, a prominent Métis leader from Regina Beach, worked to enshrine Métis rights in the Constitution. Harry had a flair for the dramatic: He greeted Pope John Paul II in Yellowknife in 1984 by taking off his jacket and presenting it to the pontiff. Nicknamed "Harry the Dog" because of his tenacity, Daniels once played Gabriel Dumont in a CBC mini-series.

DID YOU  KNOW?

Alex MacFadyen of Shaunavon has assembled a hockey scrapbook that weighs over 77 kilograms!

White Owl

By the early 1930s, conservationist Grey Owl had earned an international reputation. Films of Grey Owl and his Iroquois wife, Anahereo, in their Prince Albert National Park beaver sanctuary had been seen around the world, and Grey Owl had great success on lecture tours across North America and Europe. With his long, braided hair and fringed buckskin jacket, he was hailed as a representative of Native culture. Even the couple's pet beavers, "Jellyroll" and "Rawhide," enjoyed a certain amount of notoriety.

When Grey Owl died in Prince Albert in 1938, a furor erupted—it turned out he was actually an Englishman named "Archie Belaney"! Grey Owl's ecological message, however, resonates just as strongly today as it ever did. His story was made into a 1999 movie starring Pierce Brosnan.

A Lot of Irons in the Fire

Emma Rostron, born in 1862, immigrated to the Macrorie area, where she became the only known female blacksmith in western Canada. She met her husband, who was a blacksmith, when he bought her lunch at a box social. They worked side by side, and when he died suddenly, she carried on working in the smithy.

Extreme Gumption

Nicholas Flood Davin was a lawyer, a member of Parliament, the first person to have a literary work published in the West, and the founder of the *Regina Leader*. A larger-than-life character, Davin dressed like a dandy in top hat and cutaway coat, and he was prone to episodes of public drunkenness in a temperance town. He also carried on a torrid affair with one of his newspaper's journalists, then convinced his wife to raise his lover's child.

But perhaps Davin is best known for sneaking into jail to get an exclusive interview with Louis Riel just before the Métis rebel's 1885 execution. Davin posed as a priest coming to give Riel his last rites and managed to conduct an entire interview in French under the nose of the Anglophone guard—thereby scooping the entire world.

Petite for a Prospector

Kathleen Rice graduated as a gold medallist in mathematics from the University of Toronto in 1906. But during the gold rush, she decided to turn prospector and spent many years trapping and prospecting in the Herb Lake area. Rice Lake is named after her.

Shipwrecked

Tom Sukanen, a shipbuilder by trade, came from Finland to Minnesota early in the 20th century. In Minnesota he got married and fathered four children but couldn't make much headway as a farmer. So in 1911 he left his family in the U.S. and walked 965 kilometres to the Coteau Hills area near Macrorie, where he filed on a homestead. Sukanen was known as an ingenious neighbour, good at repairs and able to build anything, including a sewing machine and a steam-powered threshing machine.

After Sukanen had saved some money and received clear title to his homestead, he walked back to Minnesota to get his family. But when he arrived, he found the place abandoned: his wife had died, his children were scattered. He managed to locate only his son, whom he took from a foster home. Authorities stopped them at the U.S./Canada border; the son was sent to reform school, and Sukanen was deported to Canada. Heartbroken, Sukanen retreated into himself and eventually formed the idea to return to Finland—in a ship. Over the course of six years, Sukanen constructed the *Dontianen*: a boat 13 metres long and 8.5 metres high, with a keel of galvanized iron and a hull of steel.

Sukanen planned to sail up the Saskatchewan River to Hudson Bay, then on to Greenland, Iceland and Finland. Instead, he was committed to the mental hospital in Battleford, and vandals looted the ship. Sukanen died before he could see Finland again, but many parts of the *Dontianen* were salvaged, and it was rebuilt for a museum near Moose Jaw. In 1977, Sukanen's body was reinterred next to his ship.

DID YOU KNOW?

Eli Wiwcharuk of Endeavour has amassed a 31-kilogram ball of aluminum foil.

Ready for the Rapture
In 1929 a doomsday cult flourished in the community of Masefield, south of Swift Current. Followers stuck with leaders Archie and Sid Chandler for a year or two, but by the time the

brothers announced the date for the end of the world—
November 6, 1929—there were only three members left: Archie,
Sid, and Sid's wife. Newspapers reported that the three went out
to a tent in the hills to await the end. No word on what they
were doing on November 7, 1929, though.

Two-Gun Cohen

After Morris Cohen of East London was arrested for pickpock-
eting, his parents sent him to Canada to work on a farm in
Wapella. But it wasn't long before Cohen was working con
games on the west side of Saskatoon instead. At one point he
saved the life of elderly Chinese storeowner Mah Sam, and
through his friendship with the old man Cohen became
intrigued with China.

After serving in World War I, Cohen made his way to China
and got himself hired on as one of Sun Yat-sen's bodyguards!
He repeatedly risked his life against Sun's enemies, and in one
gunfight a bullet nicked his left arm. Afterward he practised
shooting with both hands at the same time—hence his nickname. Two-Gun's life of adventure didn't end in China,
though—during World War II he was a British spy and spent
some time in a Japanese prison camp.

Assmania

Dick Assman, a Regina gas station owner, became famous
briefly in the mid-1990s when *The David Letterman Show* began
making jokes about his name. Letterman introduced Assman on
his show in July 1995, and for about a month afterward featured
a nightly Assman interview. At the height of "Assmania," Dick
was asked to run for public office, serenaded by Tony Orlando
and proposed to by several women eager to become Mrs.
Assman!

I Spy

Emma Woikin, a young woman of Doukhobor origin from Blaine Lake, suffered a double tragedy when her only child died at birth and her distraught husband killed himself soon afterward. In 1942, the widow went to Ottawa alone and found work as a cipher clerk with the Department of External Affairs. While there, she met Major Sokolov, a handsome Soviet diplomat. The major seduced her with cash and expensive perfume, played on her affection for Russia—and got her to pass secret documents to him.

In 1945, a clerk at the Soviet Embassy in Ottawa—Igor Gouzenko—defected, taking with him papers that revealed Woikin and 21 others as spies. The Gouzenko Affair became one of Canada's biggest spy scandals, and the incident helped to spark off the Cold War. Emma Woikin was denounced as a traitor, charged with a breach of the Official Secrets Act, and sentenced to two-and-a-half years in the Kingston Penitentiary. After her release she moved to Saskatoon, where she worked for many years as a legal secretary.

FAVOURITE SPORTS

Statistics prove that Saskatchewan produces more NHL hockey players than any other jurisdiction. (Anyone who's been to a Roughrider game can see that the province has spawned more fanatical football fans per capita than anyplace else, too.) And when it comes to curling, skating, skiing, track, and so much more, Saskatchewan rules!

A Whole Lotta Sweeping Going On

Curling, Saskatchewan's official sport, has been popular in the province since its jam-can days. Saskatchewan's first recorded curling game was played on the North Saskatchewan River in Prince Albert in January 1882. Blocks of wood cut from tamarack trees served as the rocks.

My Rink's Bigger than Your Rink

In 1909, the Regina Curling Club built the biggest curling rink in the world, featuring nine sheets of ice. The following year—nyah, nyah, nyah-nyah, nyah—Moose Jaw built a 10-sheet rink. And the year after that, Saskatoon opened an 11-sheet rink!

World's Biggest Collection

The Turner Curling Museum in Weyburn has the largest collection of curling equipment and memorabilia in the universe. Exhibits include photos, sweaters, brooms, rocks, crests and over 18,000 curling pins.

Richardson's Round-Up

Skip Ernie Richardson, his brother Garnet and cousins Arnold and Wes won four Macdonald Briers in five years. They captured the Canadian men's curling championship in 1959, 1960, 1962 and 1963.

First in the First

The Joyce McKee rink from Saskatoon won the first-ever Canadian women's curling championship. A member of that rink was Sylvia Fedoruk—who later became Saskatchewan's first female lieutenant-governor.

Hat Trick

A rink skipped by Melfort-born Vera Pezer won three consecutive Canadian women's championships in the 1970s.

Golden Girl

Sandra Schmirler's curling team was the best female foursome of all time, winning three world championships (in 1993, '94 and '97). In 1998, Schmirler and teammates Jan Betker, Joan McCusker and Marcia Gudereit won the first-ever gold medal to be awarded for women's curling at the Nagano Winter Olympics. Sandra, whose hometown was Biggar, was dubbed "Schmirler the Curler" and "Queen of Hearts" for her three wins in the national Scott Tournament of Hearts competition. When her rink was chosen to go to the Olympics, she had just given birth to a baby. Sadly, the popular skip was diagnosed with cancer in 1999 and died in 2000 at the age of 36.

BASEBALL

A League of Their Own

Sixty-four Canadian women played in the All-American Women's Baseball League, which ran from 1943 to 1954. Of that number, 26 women were from Saskatchewan. Regina's Mary (Bonnie) Baker was the league's only woman manager. A 1992 movie starring Tom Hanks and Rosie O'Donnell brought attention to the unique chapter in sports history.

Starter

In 1975, Reggie Cleveland of Swift Current became the only
Canadian-born pitcher to start a World Series game. Cleveland
played for the St. Louis Cardinals, the Boston Red Sox and the
Milwaukee Brewers during his 13-year major league career. He
had an ERA of 4.01 in 1809 innings, with 930 strikeouts, and
a 105–106 win-loss record.

Record Smasher

Terry Puhl, a Melville native, made only 18 fielding errors in
2596 chances during his 14 seasons with the Houston Astros—
the best-ever average of any big league outfielder. He also set
a National League championship series record in 1980 when he
hit .526 against Philadelphia.

HOCKEY

The Good Old Hockey Game

At last count, over 425 Saskatchewanians have put on NHL jerseys. A few of the province's superstars include:

☛ Delisle's **Bentley Brothers.** Max Bentley (known as the "Dipsy Doodle Dandy") and his brother Doug played for the Chicago Black Hawks in the 1940s. In the 1943 season, their younger brother Reggie joined them—the first time in NHL history that three brothers made up an entire forward line. Max went on to play for the Maple Leafs, with whom he won the Stanley Cup in 1948, '49 and '51. Max racked up 544 points in his NHL career, Doug 543.

☞ **Gordie Howe** of Floral. Played 26 years with the Detroit Red Wings, and he holds the record for the most NHL regular-season games played (1767). Howe had 801 career goals, 21 all-star selections and a professional career that started in 1946 and ended in 1980. In 1966, Saskatoon held "Gordie Howe Day" in his honour.

☞ **Sid Abel** of Melville. Abel played with Howe on Detroit's "Production Line." In 1950 he and Howe were numbers two and three in the scoring race, and that year their team won the Stanley Cup.

☞ **Johnny Bower** of Prince Albert. The goalie nicknamed "The China Wall" knocked around the minor leagues until he was 34 years old, but he went on to win four Stanley Cups and to share the Vezina Trophy in 1965.

☞ **Gerry James**. The Regina-born James is the only person in history to have played for the Stanley Cup and the Grey Cup in the same season (1959 Greg Cup, Winnipeg Blue Bombers; and 1959–60 Stanley Cup, Toronto Maple Leafs).

☞ Humboldt's **Glenn Hall.** Hockey's "Mr. Goalie" was a pioneer of the "butterfly" goalie style, and he holds the record for most consecutive games played by a goaltender (502).

☞ **Brian Trottier** of Val Marie. Trottier was a member of six Stanley Cup–winning teams, including four consecutive Stanley Cups with the New York Islanders. He was the league's sixth-highest all-time scorer when he retired in 1994.

☞ Kelvington's **Wendel Clark.** Former captain of the Toronto Maple Leafs, Clark scored 46 goals in the 1994–95 season.

☞ **Theoren Fleury** from Oxbow. Fleury is the only NHL player to score three short-handed goals in a single game. He also put in a stellar performance for the gold medal–winning Canadian men's hockey team at the 2002 Salt Lake City Olympics.

☛ Shaunavon's **Hayley Wickenheiser.** *Sports Illustrated* called Wickenheiser the "best female hockey player in the world." She was a leader in the Canadian women's gold medal victory in the 2002 Olympics, and she's an Olympic-class softball player, too. After Clara Hughes, Wickenheiser was the second Canadian female to participate in both the summer and winter Olympics, and the first Canuck woman to play Olympic team sports in both seasons. Hayley was also the first woman to compete in professional men's hockey.

You Go, Girls!

Speaking of women's hockey gold, 20 percent of the 2002 women's Olympic hockey team came from Saskatchewan. Wickenheiser's teammates included Dana Antal, Colleen Sostorics and Kelly Bechard.

DID YOU KNOW?

In the 1920s, Regina had a professional hockey team. The short-lived Regina Capitals once came within one game of playing for the Stanley Cup.

Got the Blues 'Cause We Didn't Get the Blues

In 1982, Bill Hunter of Saskatoon made a bid to bring the financially strapped St. Louis Blues to his hometown. Although many commentators thought the 'Tooner was too small to support an NHL team, Hunter got commitments for 18,000 season tickets, as well as for an 18,000-seat arena. The NHL Board of Governors turned him down.

The Hounds of Notre Dame

Pere Athol Murray, a priest who ran a small college in Wilcox, led an athletic program that sent more than 100 players to the NHL, including Wendel Clark, Rod Brind'Amour and Curtis

Joseph. A 1980 movie scripted by Ken Mitchell tells the story of the good father, whose motto was *Luctor et Emergo*—"Struggle and Emerge."

From Tragedy to Triumph

Four members of the Swift Current Broncos (of the Western Hockey League) were killed in December 1986 when the team bus crashed a few kilometres from home. The Broncos went on to win the Memorial Cup in 1988–89. The only other Saskatchewan teams to win the Memorial Cup were the Regina Pats in 1974 and the PA Raiders in 1985.

Power Players

Clarence Campbell of Floral was president of the NHL for more than three decades. Dave King from Saskatoon (currently with the Columbus Blue Jackets) is considered one of the best hockey coaches in the world. And long-time *Hockey Night in Canada* broadcaster Dick Irvin was born and raised in Regina.

He Shoots, He Scores!

One of the first live broadcasts of a professional hockey game happened on March 14, 1923. CKCK radio of Regina aired the Regina Capitals–Edmonton Eskimos game.

Rink Rats

Each year the Laprairie family of Regina floods its backyard and hosts neighbourhood hockey games. In 2003, the Laprairies won CBC's *Hockey Day in Canada* contest for the country's best backyard rink.

FOOTBALL

Rider Pride

The Saskatchewan Roughriders, the oldest continuing football club in western Canada, won respect for western football by introducing the forward pass to the Grey Cup in 1929 and scoring the West's first Grey Cup touchdown in 1930.

It Was a Riot

Originally established as the "Regina Rugby Club," the team was nearly stomped when a riot broke out in 1911 after a game in Saskatoon! It was a tough game in the early days—Regina players used to throw a dollar in the pot before each game, and the first player who drew blood took the money home.

Rough

The football club's name was changed to "Roughriders" in 1924, apparently after NWMP who broke broncos (called "roughriders"). An Ottawa football team (originally in a different "union" or league) was also named "Rough Riders"—the term in the East referred to lumberjacks who rode logs down the rivers. When the two leagues merged, the CFL ended up having two teams with the same name. The "Roughriders" and the "Rough Riders" met four times to play for the Grey Cup, which made things pretty confusing for commentators. Ottawa won three of those four games, but the Ottawa team folded in 1996.

The Green and White

The team colours were red and black for many years. However, in 1948, a club executive found two sets of nylon football sweaters on sale in Chicago and bought them because the price was too good to resist—and ever since, Roughrider fans have been painting themselves green and white.

Big Gopher Terrorizes Albertans

The Roughriders' mascot is "Gainer the Gopher," a 2.4 metre tall Richardson's Ground Squirrel that pumps up the fans. The mascot's name is derived from an old cheer: "Gain some yards, ya bum!" And although Gainer once had a longish tail, it's now short—kids kept pulling the long one. The *Spermophilis richardsonii* was embroiled in a huge controversy in 2006 when the Calgary Stampeders refused to let Gainer into McMahon Stadium during a game. Apparently, the rodent's influence is just too great.

Piffles Field

The Riders' home stadium, Taylor Field, was named after an avid Regina rugby and football player named Neil "Piffles" Taylor. Taylor joined the World War I Royal Flying Corps, was shot down in France and became a prisoner of war. When he returned home he went back to football, despite having lost an eye in the war. During a game in Calgary in 1919, play had to be halted while Taylor stopped to search for his glass eye! The Roughies' home turf is now known as "Mosaic Stadium at Taylor Field."

Stowaways

In the hardscrabble days of the Depression, the football club couldn't always afford tickets for all the players to travel to away games. More than once, players hid under seats and equipment until the train got underway.

Rider fans hollow out watermelons and carve the rinds into old-fashioned football helmets, which they then wear to games.

Footloose

While playing in a particularly slippery game at Taylor Field in 1967, middle guard Ron Atchison traded his cleats for a pair of Hush Puppies, which he taped to his feet.

Grey Cup Fever

The Riders won their first Grey Cup in 1966 when they defeated the Ottawa Rough Riders 29–14. The province celebrated for days!

The Ultimate Nail-Biter

The Riders won their second Grey Cup game in 1989 when Dave Ridgway kicked a 35-yard field goal at 14:58 of the last quarter to beat the Hamilton Tiger Cats 43–40, which, incidentally, was the highest combined score in Grey Cup history!

Ridgway Rocks

Dave Ridgway holds the CFL record for most field goals in one season; he scored 59 of them in 1990. And as if that weren't enough, he also has the record for the longest field goal, 60 yards in 1987. His number, 36, has been retired by the club.

More Amazing Riders

☞ **Ron Lancaster** played a key role in Saskatchewan's first-ever Grey Cup win in 1966. His 16-year career with the Riders generated more than 20 CFL records, including 6233 passes thrown, 3384 completions and 333 touchdown passes. He also broke the record for the most games played in the CFL (288) and the most consecutive seasons in which he played every regular game (15). Lancaster's number 23 has also been retired.

☞ **George Reed** scored 137 touchdowns in 13 seasons with the Riders from 1963 to 1975, a CFL record. He also completed 16,116 yards of rushing and was the league's leading rusher nine times. He and Lancaster deserve a great deal of credit for the success of the Riders throughout the '60s and early '70s. Reed's number 32 has been retired.

☞ **Kent Austin** attempted 65 passes during a 1991 game against Edmonton. He also holds the record for the most pass attempts in one season: 770 in 1992.

☞ **Roger Aldag** from Gull Lake joined the Riders in 1976. He was named to the Western Conference All-Star Team eight times and was awarded the Schenley as the CFL's top lineman in 1986 and 1988. Aldag was one of the team's captains when it captured the Grey Cup in 1989. His number, 44, has been retired.

☞ **Vernon Vaughn** of Maryland played for the Riders between 1958 and 1960. He was the team's leading pass receiver in

1959, and at almost 2 metres tall and weighing 104 kilograms he was virtually impossible to cover. Sadly, Vaughn was diagnosed with leukemia at the age of 25 and died in 1961. One of his last requests was to be buried in his Roughrider uniform.

☛ **Glenn Dobbs,** a famous Rider of the early 1950s, generated such enthusiasm that fans renamed Regina "Dobberville." The post office even delivered mail addressed that way!

☛ **Brian Timmis,** who played for the Riders in the 1920s, once nearly choked to death on the strap of his helmet during a scrimmage. For the remainder of his career, he played helmet-less.

☛ In 1956, the team suffered a terrible loss when players Gordon Sturtridge, Mel Beckett, Ray Syrnyk and Mario Demarco were killed in a plane crash in the Rockies while returning from an all-star game in Vancouver. Their jersey numbers (73, 40, 56 and 55, respectively) have been retired. Only eight Rider numbers have been retired by the club.

"The Miracle of Taylor Field"

During a semi-final series against Calgary in 1963, the Riders made a greatly unexpected comeback. The *Edmonton Journal* headline for the article about the game read: "Snowballs Have Chance in Hell."

The Banjo Bowl

The traditional Labour Day Classic is played against the Winnipeg Blue Bombers at Taylor Field in Regina. The following weekend a rematch between the two prairie teams takes place in Winnipeg. In 2003, Bombers placekicker Troy Westwood (of Selkirk, Manitoba) was quoted as saying that

people from Regina were "a bunch of banjo-pickin' inbreds."
He later "apologized" by saying, "The vast majority of people in
Saskatchewan have no idea how to play the banjo." Since then
the rematch game has been known as "The Banjo Bowl," and the
teams play for a $10,000 prize for charity.

NFL Gridiron Greats

The NFL named Reuben Mayes of North Battleford its 1986
Rookie of the Year. During his career, "Big Rube" played for the
New Orleans Saints and the Seattle Seahawks. And Jon Ryan,
who was born, raised and still lives in Regina, is currently the
punter for the Green Bay Packers of the NFL.

SKATING

Fastest Woman on Ice

Speedskater Catriona LeMay Doan of Saskatoon won the gold medal in the 500-metre speed-skating event in the 1998 Nagano Winter Olympics—and won gold again at the 2002 Salt Lake City Olympics. LeMay Doan thus became the only Canadian to win back-to-back gold medals in the same individual event. Much to the delight of Skatchies, Doan's 1998 gold medal came on the same weekend as the Schmirler rink's gold medal curling performance. Catriona was named Canadian Female Athlete of the Year in 1998, 2001 and 2002, and received the Lou Marsh Award as Canadian Athlete of the Year in 2002.

How About Ice Fishing?

Jeremy Wotherspoon of Humboldt began speedskating to help him hone his hockey skills, but ended up at the top of the speedskating world. The most successful male skater in World Cup history, Wotherspoon won a silver medal in the 1998 Nagano Winter Olympics. He's also a world-class fly fisherman.

Go Figure!

At the age of two, when most tots are still lounging around in diapers, Trudy Treslan was skating circles around the Beechy rink. And at the age of 13, the petite redhead won the 1984 Novice Women's Figure Skating Championship with an electrifying performance in Regina.

True Grit

Norman Falkner of Saskatoon grew up near a rink and was well known about town for his figure-skating ability. Unfortunately, he was wounded in World War I and lost a leg. Determined to skate again, Falkner developed a one-legged skating technique. Although he had to be pushed onto the ice at the beginning of his performance, Falkner wowed audiences across North America with his on-ice artistry. He was also one of the world's foremost authorities on golf course ratings and handicaps, playing to an eight handicap!

RODEO

Ride 'Em, Cowboy!

More than 50 rodeos are held in Saskatchewan every year. The oldest rodeo in the province was started by the NWMP in 1890 in Wood Mountain. Generations of cowboying in Wood Mountain has paid off, as two of Saskatchewan's finest cowboys come from that area. Carl Olson won the World Saddle Bronc Championship in 1947. And steer wrestler Mark Roy won the "triple crown" in 1992: the Canadian Steer Wrestling Champion, National Finals Rodeo Steer Wrestling Average, and World Champion Steer Wrestler.

Promise Cut Short

Brian Claypool, born in the Beechy area and raised in Saskatoon, won the bull-riding title at the Calgary Stampede in 1974 and 1976. He was Canadian bull-riding champion in 1975 and '76, runner-up in '77, and set a record for most money won in a single season of bull riding in '75. Claypool won all-around cowboy awards in Oregon, Washington and Idaho, and was competing on the American circuit when he died in a plane crash in 1979.

SKIING

"Jungle Jim"

Jim Hunter, born in Shaunavon, developed an aggressive downhill ski style while in his teens and later became part of the infamous "Crazy Canuck" ski team of the 1970s. At the 1972 Sapporo Olympics, Hunter brought home a bronze medal.

Making Mountains Out of Gopher Holes

In order to bring the 1971 Canada Winter Games to Saskatoon, the city built a 91-metre "mountain" for ski events: Mount Blackstrap, near Dundurn. During construction, 371,600 cubic metres of earth were moved.

Pushing the Limits

Colette Bourgonje was the first student in a wheelchair to graduate with a degree in Physical Education from the University of Saskatchewan. Bourgonje has been recognized as one of Canada's greatest wheelchair athletes, winning medals in several ski events in four Paralympic Games, including a bronze in the 2006 Paralympics in Turin, Italy.

Downhill Granny

Marnie Winder Long of Delisle is another of Canada's finest para-athlete skiers. In the 1998 Paralympics in Nagano, Japan, she won two bronze medals and one silver one. Broadcasters couldn't get over the fact that she had grandchildren—and kept referring to her as "the grandmother"!

DID YOU KNOW?

Super Dave Osborne (comedian Bob Einstein) used to brag that his equipment featured genuine "Saskatchewan seal-skin bindings." Super Dave, by the way, is the brother of film actor and director Albert Brooks.

TRACK

"The Saskatoon Lily"

At the 1928 Amsterdam Olympics, Ethel Catherwood of Saskatoon won gold in the high jump event. That year was the first that women were considered official Olympic competitors! In 1996, Canada Post issued a stamp in Catherwood's honour.

Hurdles to Success
Earl Thomson of Birch Hills won a gold medal for Canada in the 110-metre hurdle event at the 1920 Antwerp Olympics.

No Keeping Up with Jones

In 1975, Diane Jones set a new world record in the pentathlon, with 4540 points. During her track career at the University of Saskatchewan in Saskatoon, Jones won 12 titles in four different events and was the Canadian indoor record-holder in 50-metre hurdles, long jump, shot put and pentathlon. Jones was twice ranked first in the world and would undoubtedly have excelled at the 1980 Moscow Olympics, but Canada decided to boycott the event because of the Soviet invasion of Afghanistan. Diane later married Edmonton Eskimo John Konihowski.

On the Fast Track
Harry Jerome, born in Prince Albert, became the first Canadian to officially hold a world track record at Olympic tryouts in 1960. He ran the 100-metre race in 10 seconds, a time that he eventually got down to 9.1 seconds! In 1962 a serious leg muscle injury required that Jerome spend six months in a cast, and doctors predicted he'd never run again. But Jerome recovered and won a bronze medal in the 1964 Tokyo Olympics. The Harry Jerome Track Complex opened in Prince Albert in 1992.

Clearing Hurdles

Gwen Wall Ridout of Saskatoon broke the Canadian junior 400-metre hurdles record three times, has broken 11 Canadian senior track records and at least 15 Saskatchewan track records. She made the British Commonwealth teams in 1982 and 1986, coming in fourth in Edinburgh in '86. Ridout twice represented Canada at the Pan-American Games, winning bronze in hurdles and silver with the relay team in Venezuela in 1983. One of Gwen's best times in the 400-metre hurdles was at the World Student Games in Edmonton in 1983, where she set a Canadian record of 56.10 seconds, which stood for nine years.

OTHER SPORTS

Lone Gunman Gold

In 1952, trapshooter George Generoux of Saskatoon won Canada's only gold medal at the Helsinki Olympics.

We Are the Champions

At the North American Indigenous Games, which are held in various locations and attract approximately 5000 athletes, Team Saskatchewan comes out on the top of the medal standings more often than not. At the 2006 Games, with 32 provinces and states participating, Saskatchewan garnered more than twice as many medals than Ontario, which came in second.

GOOOAAAL! (One, Anyhow)

On May 28, 1952, in Saskatoon, the Saskatchewan All-Star soccer team took on the English powerhouse team, Tottenham Hotspur F.C., in an exhibition game. The Skatchie team, which included future NHL star goalie Gump Worsley playing centre forward, was trounced by the Spurs, 18–1.

Useful Book

Nicknamed "The Moose," Earl McCready is generally regarded as the best amateur wrestler that Canada has ever produced. McCready won three Canadian heavyweight championships and was three-time U.S. national intercollegiate heavyweight champion while attending Oklahoma A&M College in the 1920s. McCready also won gold in 1930 at the first British Empire Games (forerunner to the Commonwealth Games). McCready grew up in rural Saskatchewan in Ogema, Milestone and Querrin—far from any wrestling programs. Legend has it that he learned to wrestle by studying a book called *How to Handle Big Men with Ease.*

Move Your Bunnocks

The town of Macklin doubles in size on the August long weekend, when it hosts the World Bunnock Championship Challenge. About 300 teams compete, and they come from as far away as Japan and Australia. Bunnock is a bocce-like game played with horse ankle bones, supposedly invented by bored Russian soldiers in the 1800s. It's been played in Macklin since the homesteading days. Macklin also boasts the world's biggest bunnock—9.7 metres tall—which stands on the outskirts of town.

Fore!

Per capita, Saskatchewan has more golf courses than any other jurisdiction in the world! It also boasts a higher percentage of golfers than anyplace else—33 percent of Saskatchewan residents over the age of 12 play six or more rounds of golf each season.

Does the Ball Need a Passport?

At Gateway Cities Golf Club, the first eight holes and the tee for the ninth hole are in Saskatchewan, but the final hole and the clubhouse are in North Dakota. The club straddles the communities of Portal on the U.S. side and North Portal in Canada.

"The Moose Jaw Mermaid"

Canada's female athlete of 1934, Phyllis Dewar, recorded the best performance of any Canuck at the British Empire Games in London, England—where she earned four gold medals in swimming events. She won a fifth gold medal at the Sydney British Empire Games in 1938.

Top Dogs

Canada's premier dog-sled event is the annual Canadian Challenge Sled Dog Race, a 600-kilometre marathon from Prince Albert to La Ronge. Twelve dog teams from across the world race for the Cameco Cup over the nation's longest track. The dogs wear Gore-Tex booties to keep their paws toasty.

 Saskatchewan has 10,000 kilometres of groomed and signed snowmobile trails.

Oh Deer!

Known as the "Hansen Buck," the world-record white-tailed deer was shot by Milo Hansen in November 1993, near Biggar. The buck's score was just over 213 points; its rack's inside spread measured just over 68 centimetres, and six of the rack's 10 main points exceeded 28 centimetres. More than 400 people attended the scoring ceremony at the Hansen farm.

Honestly, it was Thiiiiis Big!

Lake Diefenbaker's waters make it ideal for all kinds of water-based recreational activities. And if you happen to be a rainbow trout, the water is also an excellent environment in which to live and grow and grow and grow

Identical twins and avid anglers, Adam and Sean Konrad of Saskatoon know this and recently set out to learn just how big these fish can get.

On June 5, 2007, after weeks of persistence and numerous catches over 20 pounds, Adam informed his brother that he had something on the line that felt out of the ordinary. Twenty minutes later, the 26-year-olds had wrestled into their boat what may be the largest rainbow trout ever caught! The beast, measuring 38.5 inches in length and 34 inches around, tipped the scales at a whopping 43.6 pounds. The amazing story of this potential world-record catch even made headlines on American sports network ESPN.

Something Fishy About That
The largest lake trout in the world was caught in Lake Athabasca in August 1961. It weighed 46 kilograms.

Knockouts
Moose Jaw's Jack Reddick was the Canadian light heavyweight champion in the 1920s. And in the 1990s, Don Laliberte of Regina held the Canadian heavyweight title.

Tying a Lasso Around the World

Carmel Gowan, raised on a farm northwest of Swift Current, held the World Champion Trickroping title for many years. She toured as the half-time show for the Harlem Globetrotters and performed a renowned nightclub act in more than 80 countries, in venues such as Paris' Moulin Rouge. On tour in Vietnam in

1963, she adopted an orphan who became part of the act at an early age. Some years later, that daughter—Kim Gowan—also became the World Champion Trickroper.

Arcade-ian

Saskatoon's Greg Sakundiak set seven official world records in classic arcade games before he retired at the age of 18 in 1987. The records he set for "Dragon's Lair" (374,954 points), "Tag Team Wrestling" (3,795,500 points) and "Twin Cobra" (1,900,450 points) are mentioned in the *Guinness Book of World Records.* Sakundiak was a featured guest at the recent "Legends of the Golden Age: A Tribal Gathering of the Greatest Video Game Superstars of the 1980s" in Humble, Texas. A man of many talents, in 2003, Sakundiak was ranked fourth in the world among arm-wrestling champions!

Special Olympics

The first Saskatchewan provincial Special Olympics games were held in Regina in 1970, with 250 athletes participating. Today 1300 athletes province-wide compete in 21 sports. Saskatchewan excels at international and national levels, too. In 1986, Team Saskatchewan sent 48 athletes to the national summer games and came home with 51 medals!

That Smug 60-Year-Old Swede

In 1972, Saskatoon became the pilot community for "ParticipACTION," a federal program designed to promote physical fitness. It was a smashing success in the city, with a much-greater-than-anticipated response from all sectors of the community. The most famous ParticipACTION TV ad maintained that the average 60-year-old Swede was in better shape than a 30-year-old Canadian—which was later revealed to be a totally bogus statistic!

CRIMES AND MISDEMEANORS

A law on the books in Saskatchewan says that teenagers in Fort Qu'Appelle must have their shoelaces done up when out on the streets. Women sunbathing topless, however, are A-OK in Wascana Park. From the Wild West days to today's headlines, Saskatchewan is constantly providing colourful fodder for the law books.

Give Us Your Lupins

The first stagecoach robbery in western Canada happened near Saltcoats in July 1886 when George Garnett, a respected church-goer, robbed the mail bags of $1465.

Cypress Hills Massacre

In the spring of 1873, 17 American wolf hunters camping in the Bear Paw Mountains of Montana had their horses stolen by a party of Assiniboine from north of the border. Furious, the hunters procured more horses and rode into Canada, bent on retribution. On June 1 they came upon an encampment of Assiniboine in the Cypress Hills, and a dispute between the two groups escalated. The Americans, who were armed with Winchester and Henry rifles, fired on the Assiniboine men, women and children, killing approximately 20 and wounding many others as they fled. Eight men were tried in two separate court cases, but evidence was inconclusive and no one was ever punished for the massacre. It's generally accepted that this violent incident was a catalyst for the formation of the North West Mounted Police.

The Dickens, You Say

Francis Dickens, the third son of novelist Charles Dickens—
and regarded as lazy, alcoholic and reckless—joined the newly
formed NWMP in the 1870s. By 1885 Francis was in charge of
Fort Pitt on the banks of the North Saskatchewan River. That
spring the NWMP fought insurgents at Duck Lake. Then three
of Dickens' men went to investigate a massacre of Hudson Bay
Company employees at Frog Lake and were attacked by Cree.
The Cree very shortly surrounded Fort Pitt and suggested that
Inspector Dickens and his men might be wise to abandon their
post. This they did, jumping in a leaky scow and floating down
the river for six days until they reached Battleford.

The Last Military Conflict on Canadian Soil

In 1885, after many years of trying to obtain justice from the
Canadian government, Métis leader Louis Riel declared a provisional government at Batoche. The NWMP fought the rebels at
Duck Lake and were defeated by Gabriel Dumont's men. The
Métis next went up against the Canadian Militia at Fish Creek
and at Batoche, where they were greatly outnumbered and ulti-
mately defeated. Cree forces joined in the resistance and fought
battles at Fort Pitt, Cut Knife Hill, Frenchman's Butte, and
Steele Narrows.

Largest Mass Execution in Canadian History

Thirty-three Natives and 19 Métis were arrested for their roles
in the Northwest Resistance. In November 1885, eight of these
men were executed at a public hanging in Fort Battleford.
A special gallows was built that dropped all eight at the same
time—and the hangman was the man who had been the cook
at Frog Lake at the time of the massacre there.

The Trial of Louis Riel

Louis Riel surrendered after the Battle of Batoche and was taken to Regina where he was indicted on six counts of treason. This devout Catholic Métis visionary who led an armed uprising against Canada was tried by a six-person jury made up of English-speaking Protestants and a magistrate who was a federal employee. Despite the efforts of Riel's lawyers to convince the jury that Riel was insane, jurors found him guilty. And although the jury recommended mercy, the judge sentenced Louis to death. He was hanged in Regina on November 16, 1885.

Waist Deep in the Big Muddy

At the turn of the 20th century, the Big Muddy badlands in southwestern Saskatchewan became a haven for shady characters from the U.S. The Big Muddy was known as Station No. 1 on Butch Cassidy's famous "Outlaw Trail" that led down through Montana, Colorado, Arizona and into Juarez, Mexico. The canyons and buttes of the Big Muddy were perfect hiding places for assorted outlaws: horse thieves, cattle rustlers…and worse.

The James Gang

In 1905, Charles Parmer, reputed to be one of Jesse James' men, came to Dundurn to retire. He brought his son Earl with him, and the two set up house in a sod shack, which they lived in for decades. Parmer almost never bathed, and he slept with a revolver under his pillow every night until his death in 1935.

A Dry Cold…Very Dry

Prohibition came to Saskatchewan in 1915. In April of that year bars and clubs were forced to close by 7 PM; by July, Premier Walter Scott announced that all liquor licences were to be abolished. At the same time, the province took control of all liquor sales—thus making Saskatchewan the first province in Canada to ban private-sector sale of alcohol. During Prohibition, crime rates dropped and so did Monday-morning absenteeism. Bootlegging and rum-running, however, rose sharply. Prohibition was repealed in 1925.

Seagram's V.O.: Known by the Company it Keeps

The Bronfman family, of Seagram's Whiskey fame, reportedly got their business off to a roaring start in Saskatchewan during Prohibition. Infamous American mobster "Lucky" Luciano once remarked that "Sam Bronfman was bootlegging enough whiskey across the Canadian border to double the size of Lake Erie." Sam and Harry Bronfman's brother-in-law, Paul Matoff, was shot to death in 1922 at the Bienfait train station—apparently over a liquor deal gone wrong.

Scarface and the Jaw

Chicago gangster Al Capone, architect of the Valentine's Day Massacre in 1929, apparently masterminded a thriving rum-running business out of Moose Jaw during Prohibition. Huge tunnels under the downtown core of the city that were once used for the mobster, his henchmen and his molls have been restored and are now a tourist attraction.

Almighty Voice
In 1895 a young Cree named Almighty Voice was arrested for killing a cow and was locked in the Duck Lake jail to await trial. Apparently a guard made a joke about hanging being the penalty for slaughtering a government cow. Almighty Voice escaped and was pursued by Sergeant Colebrook of the NWMP. When Colebrook tried to arrest Almighty Voice, the fugitive

killed him with a single shot and fled. It wasn't until two years
later that authorities caught up to Almighty Voice; he and his
two companions were killed by rounds from a nine-pound field
gun near the One Arrow Reserve.

The On-to-Ottawa Trek

During the Depression, the Canadian government set up relief
camps to try to contain the many thousands of young unemployed men who were riding the rails looking for work. In the
spring of 1935, several hundred workers from rural British
Columbia went on strike—and then began a "march" (via freight
train) across the country to Ottawa. The "Trek" gathered support and momentum as it moved east. Sympathizers in towns
along the route raised money and organized meals, and more
and more young unemployed men joined the Trek at each stop.

The government grew anxious to put an end to the protest
before it reached Winnipeg—where, it was assumed, so many
men would join the Trek that it would become unstoppable.
Conspiring with the railway companies, the RCMP halted the
trains in Regina, and on July 1, 1935, the government ordered
the RCMP to use force to disperse the Trekkers. In the ensuing
violence on the city's streets, many men were injured, and two
died: a young unemployed Trekker, and a Regina city police
officer.

The Bienfait Coal Miners' Strike

On September 29, 1931, striking coal miners from Bienfait
planned a parade in Estevan to rally support for their cause. It
was a peaceful demonstration—miners brought their wives and
children, and many packed picnic lunches. The RCMP broke
up the parade by firing into the crowd, wounding approximately
20 people and killing three miners—the single greatest loss of
life of any of the confrontations of the 1930s. The three dead
miners—Peter Markunas, Nick Hargan and Julian Gryshko—

were buried under a single tombstone that read "Murdered by the RCMP."

Following the incident, 19 miners and union organizers stood trial on a variety of charges. The trials were marked by jury-tampering, perjury and blatantly biased judges. Organizer Sam Scarlett had gone into hiding near Birsay but was arrested when a letter addressed to him was intercepted. Annie Buller, a nation-ally known Communist who hadn't even been in the area at the time of the riot, was tried and convicted. Some of the immigrant miners—30 percent were from Eastern Europe, mostly from the Ukraine—were deported. However, today the union remains strong in Bienfait. Workers there have even negotiated May Day as a paid holiday, a rarity in North America.

Robin Hood of Wood Mountain

In 1902 in the Wood Mountain area, a gang of rustlers known as the "Nelson Gang" preyed on rich ranchers and redistributed the stolen cattle to struggling ranchers. However, the gang was taken over by a fellow known as "Jones," who decided to pick on small ranchers instead. Police arrested several gang members, and the rest fled to the U.S., where many met with violent ends.

"The Craziest Man in Saskatchewan"

Early in the morning of August 15, 1967, Victor Hoffman, recently released from a mental hospital, carried a .22-calibre rifle into a farmhouse near Shell Lake and shot nine members of the Peterson family at close range. Seven of the victims were children, aged one through 17. (The only survivor was four-year old Phyllis Peterson, who was sleeping under bedclothes between her two sisters and went unnoticed.) Hoffman said the devil had ordered him to commit the mass murder. Crown prosecutor Serge Kujawa called Hoffman "the craziest man in Saskatchewan." Hoffman was found not guilty by reason of insanity and died in custody in 2004.

A Miscarriage of Justice

David Milgaard, who as a teenager was convicted for the 1969 murder of Saskatoon nursing student Gail Miller, spent 23 years in jail for a crime he didn't commit. David's mother Joyce mounted a two-decade crusade to free her son, and after a 1991 Supreme Court review of his case, he was released. In 1997, DNA evidence exonerated Milgaard, and shortly afterwards another man was convicted of the crime. The Saskatchewan government issued an apology and gave Milgaard a $10-million compensation package—the largest in Canadian history.

Odd Couple

A farmer from southwestern Saskatchewan became the butt of jokes during the 1980s because of his erotic fixation on singer Anne Murray. Charles Robert Kieling was convinced the "Snowbird" diva was sending him romantic messages through his radio. Kieling has served time for violating terms of various probation orders. A play about the bizarre affair is titled *Love Is Strange*.

"Starlight Tour"

First Nations teenager Neil Stonechild was found frozen to death in 1990 on the outskirts of Saskatoon. An RCMP investigation raised suspicions that racist city police had picked up the young man and abandoned him in a deserted area on a night when the temperature plunged to -28°C. A 2003 inquiry headed by Mr. Justice David Henry Wright found the credibility of the police officers involved lacking and made several recommendations for changes to the police force's training and policies. The two police officers in question were dismissed from the force.

"Deny, Deny, Deny"

In January 1983, Joanne Thatcher Wilson, former wife of rancher and politician Colin Thatcher, was bludgeoned and then shot to death in the garage of the Regina house where she lived with her new husband. A couple of years earlier, Joanne had received $1 million in a divorce settlement from Thatcher, and the two were embroiled in a bitter custody battle over their nine-year-old daughter. Police soon linked Thatcher to the murder; he was convicted in 1984 and received a life sentence. The case, with its cast of famous characters—Colin had been the Minister of Energy in Premier Grant Devine's cabinet; his father Ross Thatcher had served as Saskatchewan's ninth premier—caused a stir far beyond the province's borders and was dramatized in a TV mini-series starring Kate Nelligan and Kenneth Welsh.

Thatcher made the news again in 1999 when it was revealed that he had been allowed to have his own horse shipped to the stables at BC's Ferndale Prison. (The facility also featured a nine-hole golf course and a tennis court.) In 2006 Thatcher was granted full parole and now lives on a ranch near Moose Jaw.

Joyriding

In the 1990s, Regina drivers were plagued by brazen car-stealing teens. Known as the "Oldsmobile Gang" for their vehicle of choice, the gang was mostly out for a good time, not a long time—96 percent of the victims got their cars back.

"Devil Church"

After a local two-year-old told her mother that she'd been abused at her daycare, Martensville police sent a rookie constable to investigate. At first the children denied anything was going on, but under further questioning they gave the officer frightening details of ritual sexual abuse. By 1992, the town was rife with rumours that a satanic cult called "The Brotherhood of the Ram" was operating in the area and that many police officers were members. Although the interrogation techniques used on the children have now been discredited, the case dragged on for several years and had a grave impact on the community.

And It Was in Vein Anyhow

In 1992 Dr. John Schneeberger of Kipling was accused of drugging and sexually assaulting two female patients. During the investigation, police drew blood from Schneeberger, but the blood DNA failed to match semen from one of the crime scenes. Eventually police plucked hair from Schneeberger's head—and bingo!—they got a DNA match.

Prior to the blood test, the doctor had apparently filled a rubber tube with someone else's blood, then performed minor surgery on himself to insert the tube into his arm—in effect creating a phony vein. Schneeberger was convicted and served two-thirds of a six-year sentence. In 2004 he was deported to South Africa for lying on his Canadian citizenship application.

"Compassionate Homicide?"

Tracy Latimer was a 18-kilogram, 12-year old quadriplegic who functioned at the level of a three-month-old. She suffered chronic pain, had been operated on repeatedly and was scheduled for more surgery. She also loved going to the circus, liked watching the horses on the family's Saskatoon-area farm and recognized family members. In October 1993, Tracy's father

Robert killed his daughter by piping carbon monoxide into the cab of his truck while she sat inside.

A jury convicted Latimer of second-degree murder, but three years later a new trial was ordered due to prosecutorial interference. The second jury also convicted Latimer, but the judge sentenced him to only two years, giving him a "constitutional exemption" to the minimum sentence. In June 2000 Latimer was sentenced to life with no possibility of parole for 10 years. Latimer declined to ask Ottawa for a pardon, his only legal recourse at that point.

The Fugitive and Mr. and Mrs. Smith

In July 2005, two RCMP officers were shot during a high-speed pursuit near Mildred, a tiny community in the Spiritwood area. The suspect, Curtis Dagenais, then escaped into the countryside. A massive week-long manhunt with officers, dogs, planes and helicopters failed to flush him out. Meanwhile, both officers died in hospital. Early in the morning on the 11th day after the shootings, a local farm couple named Smith found Dagenais asleep in the cab of their tractor. They took him back to their house and over the course of six hours talked Dagenais into riding with them to the Spiritwood RCMP detachment to surrender.

In the Arms of Morpheus

Kim Walker, a welder from the Yorkton area, shot his daughter's boyfriend to death on St. Patrick's Day 2003. Walker's defense recalled the old Wild West adage, "He needed killing"—Walker alleged that the boyfriend had led his 16-year-old daughter into a life of addiction and was supplying her with morphine. Although Walker's daughter considers her father a hero, a 2007 jury found him guilty of murder.

LEGAL EAGLES

Mountie School

Canada's only RCMP training academy is located in Regina. "Depot" has been training cadets since the establishment of the mounted police in 1885. The first musical ride took place on-site in 1887.

DID YOU KNOW?

Elsie Hall was the first female graduate from the University of Saskatchewan College of Law, Class of 1920.

Doukhobor Lawyer

Peter Makaroff was the first Doukhobor in the world to receive a university degree and to enter a profession. He graduated from the University of Saskatchewan College of Law in 1918. He later defended some of the On-to-Ottawa Trekkers charged in the Regina Riot of 1935 and devoted much of his life to promoting world peace.

Pioneer Judge

Ethel MacLachlan became the first female judge and the first juvenile court judge in the province in 1917. For the next 18 years, MacLachlan handled more than 5000 cases annually, and she travelled approximately 40,000 kilometres per year. She was also the first woman in Canada to be appointed a justice of the peace.

And There Were No Doughnut Shops Back Then, Either

For more than a decade in the 1900s, Saskatchewan had a provincial police force. Due to wartime shortages, the RCMP withdrew from policing the province, and 45 detachments of the

Saskatchewan Provincial Police (SPP) took over. The first 50 cops on the beat had no uniforms, no firearms and no transportation! Although the force successfully battled a post–World War I crime wave, the SPP force was disbanded in 1928, and all policing responsibility was handed back to the RCMP.

Eminent Emmett

Emmett Hall served as chief justice of Saskatchewan and later on the Supreme Court of Canada. He was the chairman of the Royal Commission on Health Services in the early 1960s and wrote the report that recommended that Canada adopt a universal health care system.

CSI: Regina

Dr. Frances McGill was the first woman to become a member of the RCMP. From 1928 to 1948, she helped solve hundreds of cases using forensic science. Her ingenious and ground-breaking methods earned her the nickname "Saskatchewan Sherlock Holmes."

Fighting for the Underdog

Dianne Martin, born in Regina, was a co-founder of The Innocence Project, a York University program that uses DNA evidence to exonerate the wrongly convicted. The project led to the vindication of Romeo Phillion in 2003, who had been imprisoned for 32 years on a conviction of murder.

Hail to the Chief

Brian Dickson of Yorkton was the chief justice of the Supreme Court of Canada from 1984 to 1990.

STRANGE LAWS

See You in "Cowrt"

Some bovine-related laws used to be on the books in Saskatchewan: In Jasmine it was illegal for a cow to moo within 300 metres of a private home. In Bladworth it was illegal to frown at cows. And it's still against the law to put graffiti on someone else's cow—though it's legal to decorate your own.

Not the Good Old Days
In a spectacularly racist and sexist move in 1912, the Saskatchewan Legislature made it illegal for European-Canadian women to work for businesses owned by Chinese men.

Estate Planning

In June 1948, farmer Cecil Harris became accidentally pinned beneath his tractor. Afraid he might perish, Harris scratched his will onto the tractor's rear fender with his jackknife: "In case I die in this mess, I leave all to the wife. Cecil Geo. Harris." Ten days later, some neighbours found him, but Harris died of his injuries shortly afterwards. The etched fender was admitted to probate as a legal holographic will. It was on "file" at the Kerrobert Courthouse until 1996, when it was moved to the University of Saskatchewan's Law Library.

Jurisdiction, Jurisdiction, Who's Got the Jurisdiction?
In the town of Lloydminster, which straddles the border between Saskatchewan and Alberta, a motorist could conceivably run a Saskatchewan red light, but experience the resulting collision in Alberta.

Saskatchewan Means Having to Say You're Sorry
A pending amendment to Saskatchewan's Evidence Act will remove the legal implications of an apology.

ARTSY-FARTSY

*Saskatchewan established the first arms-length arts board in
North America in 1948. And the province leads the country in
arts and culture volunteerism, contributing two million volunteer
hours per year. These things may have something to do with the
amazing amount of creative activity in the province. Of course,
those long winters probably help, too...*

Music, Music, Music

The funky Regina Folk Festival, the eclectic SaskTel
Saskatchewan Jazz Festival and the bootscootin' Craven
Country Jamboree attract the biggest names in music and
thousands of fans. Every year there are dozens of music events
in Saskatchewan: the Saskatoon Blues Festival, Ness Creek
Folk Festival, Govan Fiddle Festival, Northern Lights Bluegrass
Festival, the Carlton Trail Jamboree, the Wood Mountain
Stomp, just to name a few. And who could forget oom-pah—
all those polka festivals! In 2007 two of Canada's most famous
music awards shows were held in Saskatchewan: the Juno
Awards (and Nelly Furtado) came to Saskatoon, and Regina
hosted the Canadian Country Music Awards.

No Clouds in Her Way

Joni Mitchell is one of the biggest names in music. She's recorded
nine gold albums, her songs have been covered by a huge variety
of singers, and her work has influenced a generation of young
singers and songwriters. Roberta Joan Anderson was born in
Alberta, but her family moved to Saskatchewan soon afterwards,
eventually settling in Saskatoon. As a teenager Joni taught herself
to play the ukulele, learned a few folk songs and tried to land
some gigs. (The local folkie hotspot, the Louis Riel coffee house
on Broadway, initially turned her down!) And although Mitchell
left Saskatchewan early in her career, here's some evidence to
suggest that Saskatchewan has never really left her:

- At her first appearance at Carnegie Hall, Joni greeted the audience by saying, "It's a long way from Saskatoon, Saskatchewan, to Carnegie Hall."

- On the self-portrait on the cover of her album "Clouds," Joni is shown holding a western red lily, Saskatchewan's emblem.

- The iconic song "Raised on Robbery" was written about— and in—Regina's Empire Hotel.

- Although she's long been based in California, Mitchell is occasionally spotted on visits home to Saskatoon, attending the Shakespeare on the Saskatchewan Festival, or relaxing with friends at Lydia's Pub.

Up Where She Belongs

Born on the Piapot reserve in the Qu'Appelle Valley, Cree musician and activist Buffy Sainte-Marie became famous in the 1960s as a Native activist and a writer of protest songs. "Universal Soldier" became an anthem of the peace movement, and she was blacklisted by the Johnson White House. But during the same era, her love song "Until It's Time for You to Go" was recorded by Elvis, Barbra Streisand and Cher. For several years Sainte-Marie was a regular on *Sesame Street* (along with her son, Dakota). The song "Up Where We Belong," co-written by Sainte-Marie for the film *An Officer and a Gentleman,* won an Academy Award in 1983.

Musical Mentor

In 1968, Don Freed of Saskatoon sang one of his songs on film for The Man in Black in the documentary *Johnny Cash: The Man, the World, and His Music.* And although he spent many years touring and collaborating with top recording artists, Freed, who is of Métis ancestry, has spent the past decade helping Native and Métis youth to create their own music. *Our Very Own Songs*, an album created with elementary students from 28 northern communities, has been a big hit with Saskatchewan children.

Our History in Song

Edith Fulton of Lumsden, one of Canada's best-known folklorists, collaborated with Alan Mills to write a series of programs for CBC Radio called "Canada: A History in Song." The resulting record was named one of the best recordings of 1956 by the *New York Times.*

The King of Country

Ameen "King" Ganam, who was born to a Lebanese immigrant family in Swift Current, was playing the fiddle for dances by age nine. He went on to form his own band and hosted radio and television shows in the 1950s and early '60s. Ganam was one of the inaugural inductees into the Canadian Country Music Hall of Fame.

Rock On

Saskatchewan's most successful touring rock band was Streetheart, formed in Regina in 1976. Hit songs included "Action," "Hollywood," "Look in Your Eyes" and a cover version of the Rolling Stones' "Under My Thumb."

Catch of the Day

Saskatoon's Northern Pikes scored huge hits in the early 1990s with "She Ain't Pretty," "Girl with a Problem," and "Kiss Me, You Fool." They also wrote and sang the theme song for the CBC-TV show *Due South*.

Two Kinds of Music: Country AND Western

Some of country music's favourite acts come from Saskatchewan, including the Johner Brothers from Midale, and Gary Fjellgaard, originally from Rose Valley.

Agronomicon

And we shouldn't forget Porksword, a rockin' band whose specialty was twisted small-town tales such as "Intercontinental Tractor Pull Champion," "Stu's Farm" and "Medichair Run Amok." The band members—Graham Poop, Don Knutts, Spacebar, and Steve Jodrell—often made reference to Skatchie haunts, such as the Saskatoon country bar the Texas T. Their album *Agronomicon* featured a picture of a cow in front of a Pool elevator and was released by Combine Records.

DID YOU KNOW?

Regina-born Colin James' self-titled blues/swing/rock album of 1988 was Canada's fastest-selling album of all time.

The Music Man

Frank Laubach, who emigrated from Scotland to Canada in 1904, was a busy guy:

☛ He organized and conducted the Regina Orchestral Society (forerunner of the Regina Symphony).

☛ He helped to organize the first competitive provincial music festival.

☛ He taught violin at the University of Regina's music department.

☛ He conducted a dance orchestra and a 600-voice children's choir.

☛ He composed church music, opera and marches—including the piece "The Saskatchewan," to celebrate the province's inauguration in 1905.

Giant Slalom Beethoven

The Regina Symphony Orchestra holds a performance of classical music every August on a ski hill in Buffalo Pound Provincial Park.

We'll Need a Lot of Phentex

Regina singer and songwriter Connie Kaldor was once called "indecently talented" by the *Toronto Star.* She is known for her beautifully crafted songs in a variety of styles and also for her irreverent humour. Kaldor says now that the old prairie elevators are coming down, she's hoping some Ukrainian grandmothers in Saskatchewan will decide to crochet gigantic toilet-roll covers for those ugly inland grain terminals.

Lend Me a Tenor

John Vickers of Prince Albert is widely acknowledged as one of the greatest operatic tenors of his generation. After several years of singing at churches and in amateur productions on the Prairies, Vickers won a scholarship to Toronto's Royal Conservatory of Music. He went on to the Covent Garden Company at London's Royal Opera House, and then to the Metropolitan Opera, where he remained for 20 seasons, playing 116 roles. He also sang at Milan's La Scala, in Paris, Bayreuth and Salzburg, before retiring in 1988. His strong moral and religious beliefs sometimes led Vickers to take controversial stands, such as refusing to sing the title role in Wagner's "Tannhauser."

Saskatchewan Idol

Theresa Sokyrka of Saskatoon was the runner-up in the 2004 *Canadian Idol* competition. Her album *These Old Charms* debuted at number four on the charts and later went gold. Theresa attended Ukrainian bilingual elementary school and wrote her first song when she was four. It was called "When Chickens Climb Up Ladders."

Singing for Other Peoples' Suppers

Tom Jackson, born on the One Arrow Reserve, is well known for his portrayal of Chief Peter Kinidi on the television drama *North of 60.* Jackson, who's also an accomplished singer, has helped to raise more than $9 million for food banks, disaster relief and family service agencies over the years.

You Can't Say Saskatchewan Without "ska"

When you think of Saskatchewan, "ska" music doesn't jump immediately to mind. But Regina's Skavenjah, one of North America's premiere ska bands, is skanking up the province with their own version of the reggae-style pop sound! Their most recent album went to number one in Guadalajara, Mexico.

Saskatoon, Apparently

Susan Jacks, one half of the '70s pop duo The Poppy Family, was born Susan Pesklevits in Saskatoon. She and husband Terry had hits with "Where Evil Grows" and "Which Way You Goin', Billy?" which hit number one in Canada, number two in the U.S. and sold 2.5 million copies.

Megamunch

Brenda Baker of Saskatoon has recorded three very successful albums for kids, including one called *Megamunch and Other Singable Songs*. Megamunch is the half-sized robotic T. Rex that lives at the Royal Saskatchewan Museum!

Sax-y Guy

The world's most-recorded saxophonist is Paul Brodie, who began his musical career playing the clarinet in the Regina Lions Band. Paul has played for many films, as well as providing the soundtrack for Warren Beatty's sax-playing in the movie *Heaven Can Wait*.

Ca-na-da, We Love Thee…and Malaysia, Too

Bobby Gimby, best known as the "Pied Piper" who composed the 1967 Canadian Centennial song, was born in Cabri, Saskatchewan. The sheet music for the song sold an amazing 75,000 copies. Gimby also wrote the Malaysian national anthem, "Malaysia Forever"!

WRITING

Poets Laureate

The Saskatchewan Poet Laureate Program, the first of its kind in Canada, was established in 2003. The first three poets to hold the position were:

- ☛ Glen Sorestad (2003–04)

- ☛ Louise Halfe (2005–06)

- ☛ Robert Currie (2006–)

Cowboy Poet

The most famous of Saskatchewan's cowboy poets was Bill Gomersall, who died in March 2006—just 12 hours short of his 101st birthday. Bill was a working cowboy who raised horses and rodeo stock in the Mayberry district. He performed at rodeos, fairs and "chautauquas"—the variety shows that flourished between World War I and the Great Depression. And he also performed at Moose Jaw's Festival of Words at the age of 100.

That's a Lotta Words

Speaking of which, the annual Festival of Words has presented more than 375 performers to more than 19,000 people since its inception in 1997. Presenters read like a Who's Who of Can. Lit., including Margaret Atwood, Alistair MacLeod, Nino Ricci, Susan Musgrave, Jane Urquhart and David Adams Richards. The festival is accompanied by a free five-day writing workshop for teens, and a Books For Kids program, which gives away books written by Canadian authors.

Da Guild

The Saskatchewan Writers Guild, founded in 1969, is one of Canada's largest writers' organizations, boasting more than 500 members. It runs many programs, but the most popular are the writers/artists colonies at beautiful locations such as Christopher Lake and St. Peter's Abbey, where scribblers and their visual arts cousins from across the country can find a bit of peace and quiet to ply their crafts.

B Is for Best-Seller

Kids across Canada have been introduced to Saskatchewan by Jo Bannatyne-Cugnet's *A Prairie Alphabet*. Illustrated by Yvette Moore, the book celebrates harvest meals in the field, Agribition, dugouts, sundogs, quonsets, and even wind. The book went through an extraordinary five printings in its first year and to date has sold over 200,000 copies. It also inspired a symphony, composed by Regina's Elizabeth Raum.

Saskatchewan has, per capita, more Governor General's Award winners in literature than any other province.

Other Noted Wordsmiths

☛ **W.O. Mitchell** is best remembered for *Who Has Seen the Wind* (1934) and the *Jake and the Kid* series. Born and raised in Weyburn, Mitchell's inspiration often came from his love of the prairie landscape. For many years Mitchell was regarded as the voice of Saskatchewan.

☛ **Wallace Stegner,** the great American novelist, spent part of his childhood in the Cypress Hills region near Eastend. His book *Wolf Willow,* "a history, a story, and a memory of the last plains frontier," is set there. The one-and-a-half storey house built by Stegner's father in 1916 has now been turned into a writers' retreat in Eastend.

☛ **Sinclair Ross,** born on a farm near Shellbrook, worked for 40 years at the Royal Bank. In his spare time, he wrote the Canadian classic *As For Me and My House,* about the Depression on the Prairies, but he's also often remembered for his short story about the farmer who dies in a blizzard, "The Painted Door."

☛ **Max Braithwaite**, born in Nokomis, was best known for a book about teaching in a one-room schoolhouse in Saskatchewan during the Depression. *Why Shoot the Teacher?* was made into a 1977 film starring Bud Cort and Samantha Eggar.

☛ **Ken Mitchell**'s body of work includes more than 20 books, a score of stage plays, plus screenplays and teleplays. One of his best-known stage plays is *Cruel Tears,* Mitchell's prairie take on *Othello,* which featured country music by Humphrey and the Dumptrucks.

☛ **Guy Vanderhaeghe** won the Governor General's Award for Fiction for *Man Descending* in 1982, and for *The Englishman's Boy* in 1996. The latter was also short-listed for the Booker Prize. Vanderhaeghe's book *The Last Crossing* was chosen as the winner in the 2004 "Canada Reads" competition on

CBC. Born in Esterhazy, Vanderhaeghe lives in Saskatoon with his wife, artist Margaret Vanderhaeghe.

- **Sharon Butala,** who lives near Eastend, is known for her explorations of land, people and spirit. Her non-fiction book *The Perfection of the Morning* reached number one on the best-seller list. In 1996, Sharon and husband Peter Butala donated their 13,100-acre ranch near Eastend to the Nature Conservancy of Canada to establish The Old Man on His Back Prairie and Heritage Preserve.

- **Maria Campbell** was born in Park Valley. Her 1973 autobiography *Half-Breed* recounted her harrowing early experiences and sounded a call for a renewal of pride in Métis history and heritage. She lives on Gabriel Dumont's old homestead and continues to write and work for social justice.

- **Alistair MacLeod,** winner of the IMPAC Dublin Literary Award for his Cape Breton–based novel *No Great Mischief,* spent much of his childhood in Saskatchewan.

- **Will James** is often credited with creating the myth of the American cowboy…but it turns out that he was really Ernest Dufault, a Québecker who ranched near Val Marie. Hollywood turned several of James' novels into movies.

- **Walter Farewell,** an impoverished jack of all trades and erstwhile bootlegger, died in obscurity in Edam in 1955. After his death, three notebooks of blunt and colourful verse were discovered in his shack. The poems paint a vivid picture of early Saskatchewan.

- **Sylvia Legris** of Saskatoon won the prestigious and lucrative 2006 Griffin Poetry Prize for her third volume of poetry, *Nerve Squall.*

- **Arthur Slade** of Cypress Hills won the 2001 Governor General's Award for Children's Literature, for *Dust.* He also writes *Great Scott!*—a comic superhero who is "stronger than a cup of Tim Horton's coffee."

VISUAL ART

Picture Perfect

Courtney Milne of Grandora has taken more than 475,000 luminous photographs of planet earth. After a 10-month tour of all seven continents, he created a series of books called *The Sacred Earth,* and presented a slide show at the United Nations "Earth Summit" in Rio de Janeiro in 1992 that featured some of the 60,000 photos from his project. Milne has also published three books of closer-to-home photographs: *Prairie Light, Prairie Dreams* and *Prairie Skies.*

Setting Up Camp

In 1936, the University of Saskatchewan set up the Emma Lake Artists' Workshop in the province's northern boreal forest. Spearheaded by art professor Augustus Kenderdine, the workshop was an immediate success. The amazing thing is that it happened at all: 1936 was the height of the Depression. Kenderdine said he hoped "to let the young people of Saskatchewan see beauty in a land that men were becoming to hate as a place of darkness and defeat." Emma Lake remains a world-renowned artists' retreat.

The Drawing Nun

Louis Riel's sister Sara was one of the first Métis women to join the mission of Sisters of Charity (Grey Nuns). Sara Riel did charity work in the Ile-A-La-Crosse region for many years, and some of her onionskin drawings of the village still survive.

Colouring on the Walls

Moose Jaw's downtown boasts almost 40 murals. Ceramic tiles, bas-relief and paint adorn walls with images such as breaking sod with an ox, a Native shaman, the old CPR station, baseball teams of the 1930s and '40s, a pioneer woman with a cow, a threshing bee and the Sprigs o' Heather all-girls pipe band.

Counting on Art

Count Berthold Imhoff was born into nobility on a castle on the Rhine in 1868. In an attempt to escape the effects of industrialization, the classically trained painter came to St. Walburg in 1914. Until his death at the age of 71, Imhoff painted hundreds of religious works in the style of Renaissance artists. Many Saskatchewan churches commissioned his works, but sometimes Imhoff refused payment—as he did with the 80 life-sized figures and frescoes at St. Peter's Cathedral in Muenster, which took him an entire year to complete.

Driven to Abstraction

William Perehudoff of Langham is one of Canada's major figures in abstract art and the country's leading colourfield painter. He got his professional start in the late 1940s while working as a labourer in Fred Mendel's Saskatoon meat-packing plant—Mendel commissioned Perehudoff to paint a series of murals about the meat-packing process for the plant's cafeteria walls!

Life Is in the Details

Ernest Lindner, born in Vienna, immigrated to Saskatoon in the 1920s. His art often depicted the microscopic details of nature. One of Saskatchewan's most influential artists, Lindner held weekly gatherings of artists and thinkers at his home for some 30 years, a ritual that became known as "Saturday Nights at Ernie's."

Bay Street Cattle Drive

Joe Fafard, born and raised near the French-Métis community of Ste. Marthe, is best known for his sculptures of cows. Recognized as one of Canada's best visual artists, and with exhibitions in every major gallery in the country, Fafard has seven oversized cows on display at the Toronto-Dominion Centre in Toronto.

Home Sweet Home

Graham Patterson of Woodrow is, at 26, the youngest artist to sell a work to the National Gallery in Ottawa. His uniquely Saskatchewan creation "Woodrow" is a large diorama-like installation version of his hometown, complete with a hockey rink, a farmhouse, an elevator and a church. It's populated by miniature hockey teams and videos of stop-action animated puppets—some of which are modelled on Patterson's relatives.

Within His Heart

Allen Sapp is well known for his paintings of everyday reserve life. He won the Governor General's Award in 2003 for his illustrations for the children's book *The Song Within My Heart*. Sapp is a descendent of Chief Poundmaker and was raised by his grandmother, Maggie Soonias, on the Red Pheasant Reserve. The Allen Sapp Gallery–Gonor Collection in North Battleford is the only public gallery in Canada dedicated to the work of a living artist.

Make a Joyful Art

Vic Cicansky quit school in grade nine to work as a carpenter. Instead, he became a sculptor whose pieces have given delight to art audiences across the continent. Cicansky's work includes a series of outhouse sculptures, a Volkswagen series, and most famously, a series of jar sculptures.

Saskatchetoons

Dave Geary of Saskatoon, a.k.a. "Dr. Cartoon," has a line of greeting cards that spotlight characters such as Saskatoon Berry Boy, the Enchanted Albino Gopher, and Arty the Wannabe Prairie Beatnik Poet.

Hard To Be Bad

Moose Jaw artist Johann Wessels created a prop painting for Season 2, Episode 7 of the sitcom *Corner Gas*. The painting depicted a demented-looking gopher holding a hockey stick.

THEATRE

Live Entertainment

For early rural settlers in the province, chautauquas provided a welcome relief from back-breaking farm chores. "Chautauquas" were travelling shows that included musical numbers, plays, magic and puppet shows—and educational lectures covering every topic from current events to travel to temperance. Now, with 86 community theatre groups throughout the province and several world-class professional theatres, entertainment is everywhere!

First Drama Department

In 1945, the Department of Drama was established at the University of Saskatchewan. At the time, Professor Emrys Jones was the first full-time professor of drama at a Commonwealth university, and the department was the only one in Canada "devoted solely to the teaching of drama." One of the first graduates of the department was Frances Hyland.

Royal Audience

Rex Deverell served as playwright-in-residence at the Globe Theatre in Regina for 15 years: a Canadian record! The Globe is the only fixed theatre-in-the-round in Canada. And in the mid-1990s, His Royal Highness Prince Edward became a patron of the theatre—the first time he'd bestowed patronage in Canada. The prince has attended the theatre twice.

Fringe Element

An early play at Saskatoon's 25th Street Theatre was called *If You're So Good, What Are You Doing in Saskatoon?*—but the theatre's best-known work was *Paper Wheat,* a popular collective drama with music that explored the origins of the Saskatchewan Wheat Pool. The theatre produces the Saskatoon Fringe Festival, one of the most successful theatre festivals in the West.

PERFORMERS

Stars of the Land of Living Skies

☛ **Frances Hyland** (1927–2004), born in Shaunavon, made her professional stage debut in 1950 in London, England, as Stella in *A Streetcar Named Desire* (playing opposite John Gielgud). She also starred in the classic Canadian film *The Drylanders,* about the dust bowl on the Prairies—which was the first English-language feature-length film released by the National Film Board.

☛ **Shirley Douglas,** daughter of Saskatchewan's longest-serving premier Tommy Douglas, is one of Canada's best-loved performers. Her roles include Hagar Shipley, Nellie McClung, and Ma Bailey in *Wind At My Back.* In 1997 she starred onstage in *The Glass Menagerie* with her son Kiefer Sutherland.

☛ **Gordon Tootoosis**' first film role was in *Alien Thunder,* which also starred Marlon Brando, Charlton Heston and Chief Dan George. Gordon's other films include *Big Bear, Legends of the Fall* and the animated Disney film *Pocahontas.* He also played "Albert" in *North of 60.* Tootoosis still lives on the Poundmaker First Nation, near Battleford.

☛ Actor and director **Henry Woolf**'s amazing film credits include *The Rocky Horror Picture Show, Marat/Sade, The Lion in Winter* and *Gorky Park.* A life-long friend of Nobel Prize–winning playwright Harold Pinter, Woolf commissioned and starred in Pinter's first play. Woolf also directed the North American premiere of Pinter's more recent play, *Ashes to Ashes,* in Saskatoon.

☛ **John Vernon** (1932–2005) was born Adolphus Raymundus Vernon Agopsowicz in Regina, where his acting career began at the Regina Little Theatre. He went on to star on

Broadway and at the Stratford Festival and then to fame in Hollywood. His films include *Dirty Harry, Animal House* and Alfred Hitchcock's *Topaz*. He's also remembered for his starring role in the wildly successful 1960s CBC-TV drama series *Wojeck*.

☞ Tony Award–winning **Arthur Hill** (1922–2006) was born in Melfort. He starred as "George" in the original Broadway production of *Who's Afraid of Virginia Woolf?* and went on to act in film and television. His most famous role was as the title character in the 1970's TV series *Owen Marshall: Counselor at Law.*

☞ **Kim Coates** of Saskatoon has over 40 films to his credit, including *The Island, Waterworld, The Client, Open Range, Pearl Harbour* and *Black Hawk Down*. Coates has also been seen on TV series such as *Miami Vice, Lonesome Dove* and *CSI: Crime Scene Investigation.*

Cameos

And a few others who passed through the province briefly:

☞ **Peter Gzowski** (1934–2002) was once the city editor of the *Moose Jaw Times-Herald*. The iconic *Morningside* radio host broadcast his last show from Moose Jaw in May 1997.

☞ **Leslie Nielsen** was born in Regina, although his RCMP officer father soon moved the family to the Yukon. Nielsen achieved fame as a serious actor in film and television in the 1950s and '60s but found his true calling as a comedic actor in films such as *Airplane!* and *The Naked Gun.*

☞ **Art Linkletter** was born in Moose Jaw. Abandoned by his parents, he was adopted by a preacher who moved the family to the U.S. Linkletter was the host of two of the longest-running shows in broadcast history: *House Party* and *People Are Funny*. He also interviewed children for *Kids Say the Darndest Things.*

FILM AND TELEVISION

Still Running

The Yorkton Short Film and Video Festival is the longest-running festival of its kind in North America. Entries for the first festival in 1950 came from Canada, India, Brazil, Denmark, Australia, Switzerland, Sweden, the United States and Britain. The festival now draws a yearly average of 375 entries.

Documentary Pioneer

Evelyn Spice-Cherry of Yorkton was one of the founding members of the National Film Board (NFB) and made more than 128 films for the NFB. In the late 1940s, Spice-Cherry was fired due to the "red scare" and assertions that her films showed a left-wing slant.

And the Oscar Goes to...

Darwin Peachey, Saskatchewan born and raised, was one of seven people at Pixar Animation Studios to receive an award from the Academy of Motion Picture Arts and Sciences in 1993. Peachey helped to develop software that's used in the animation industry—including such popular kids' flicks as *Toy Story* and *Cars*.

Ready for a Close-Up

Movies shot in Saskatchewan include:

☛ ***Paperback Hero*** (1973), starring Keir Dullea and Elizabeth Ashley.

☛ ***Alien Thunder*** (1974), starring Chief Dan George, Donald Sutherland and Gordon Tootoosis.

- *Who Has Seen the Wind* (1977), directed by Allan King and starring Gordon Pinsent.

- *Grey Owl* (1999), directed by Richard Attenborough and starring Pierce Brosnan.

- *Tideland* (2005), directed by Monty Python's Terry Gilliam and starring Jennifer Tilly.

- And the upcoming *3 Day Test,* directed by Corbin Bernsen, was filmed in Kipling, the town that traded a house for a role in the movie!

- Some downright weird-sounding movies made in Saskatchewan: *Land of the Yodelling Mushroom People, Holiday at Waskesiu, The Stuff That Makes You Lift Cars, Gone Curling* and *They Live to Polka*.

TV Guide

Notable TV specials shot in Saskatchewan:

- *The Hounds of Notre Dame* (1980), starring Thomas Peacocke and Frances Hyland.

- *Love and Hate* (1989), starring Kate Nelligan and Kenneth Welsh.

- *Big Bear* (1998), starring Gordon Tootoosis.

- *Without Malice* (2000), starring Jennifer Beals.

- *Try to Remember* (2004), based on a Mary Higgins Clark novel, starring Gabrielle Anwar.

CORNER GAS

It's a Gas, Gas, Gas!

Corner Gas, the sitcom set in the fictional town of Dog River, Saskatchewan, debuted in January 2004. The first episode drew 1.2 million viewers, and ratings now average 1.6 million. The "Merry Gasmas" Christmas episode had a viewing audience of 3 million.

Now Everybody's Gonna See It

In 2007 the series was syndicated, which means that people all over the world will get a chance to experience life in Dog River. And American cable network superstation WGN has picked up *Corner Gas,* making it available to 70 million U.S. homes.

DID YOU KNOW?

Tales from Dog River, a trivia book about *Corner Gas,* passed the 2006 Giller prize winner on the best-seller list.

Home Boys and Girl

Three of the lead actors on *Corner Gas* are from Saskatchewan:

☛ **Brent Butt** is from Tisdale. He was born on August 3, 1966—the same day that comic Lenny Bruce died. Brent is one of Canada's hottest stand-up comedians and is the driving force behind the show. He has flat feet, is fascinated with sasquatch and as a child was once thrilled to hear Daffy Duck say "Saskatchewan" on TV.

☛ **Eric Peterson** is from Indian Head. His sister Barbara runs a bed and breakfast near Katepwa Lake. Eric is well known as one of the regulars on *Street Legal,* but he's also one of theatre's biggest names. Eric and playwright John Gray co-wrote *Billy Bishop Goes to War,* a musical about the Canadian World War I flying ace that went to London, Edinburgh and Broadway. Peterson played 18 characters in the play. Eric is a vanilla ice cream addict.

☛ **Janet Wright,** her sister Susan and her then-husband Brian Richmond founded Persephone Theatre in Saskatoon in 1975. They named the theatre after the Greek goddess of the fruitful earth, in the hopes it would thrive on the prairie—which it continues to do. Janet was once in a film with Katharine Hepburn and has also worked with Mark Wahlberg and George Clooney. She collects ceramic pigs. Janet Wright and Eric Peterson have known one another for 35 years, since their student days at the University of Saskatchewan.

Acapulco, Paris, Rouleau...

The *Corner Gas* series is filmed in the village of Rouleau (Saskatchewan's first one-million bushel town). The popularity of the sitcom has boosted tourism in Rouleau (a.k.a. "Dog River"), with about 300 visitors a day coming through during filming season.

Joe Eyebrow

Characters on *Corner Gas* often have last names that are the same as Saskatchewan towns: Lacey *Burrows,* Wanda *Dollard,* Hank *Yarbo,* Brent *Leroy,* Davis *Quinton,* Karen *Pelly.* One name you probably won't be hearing, though, is "Melfort." Apparently Melfort is the model for Dog River's despised rival town, "Wullerton."

Can't Get Enough of Saskatchewan

Corner Gas is getting a little competition in the "Sitcoms from Saskatchewan" department—*Little Mosque on the Prairie* debuted in January 2007 to a massive audience of over 2 million! The series, created by comedienne Zarqa Nawaz, attracted international attention before its premiere and was featured on newscasts on CNN and in the British media, as well as in the *New York Times.*

TRADITIONAL RITUALS

Socializing on the Prairies was harder to do than anywhere else—your nearest neighbour might be miles away, and getting there, especially in winter, was no picnic. So when folks did get together, they made sure to have a good time. Some of the old Saskatchewan traditions are dying out, but some are just as strong as ever—and once in a while a new one springs up!

The Fowl Supper

In October in Saskatchewan, when harvest is over, communities gather at halls and church basements for the annual fowl supper. Local cooks—often the women on the hospital auxiliary—bring turkey and all the trimmings: mashed potatoes, coleslaw, home-made buns, jellied salads and pies. (And if you're lucky, maybe perogies and cabbage rolls, too.) Conversation is lively and the clean-up crew in the kitchen is always busy. If you've got a hankering to throw your own fowl supper, here are directions for a couple of perennial favourites:

☞ **Jellied Salad**. Jellied salads became popular at community suppers in the 1950s because they were a status symbol. You see, you can't make a jellied salad unless you have a refrigerator, and after rural electrification began in 1948, bringing a jellied salad proved that you had a pricey electric ice-box. The salad's popularity seems to be on the wane, but here's hoping it makes a comeback.

To make it, just follow the directions on a package of lemon or lime Jell-O. Put it in the fridge until it starts to set (about an hour). Then let your imagination go wild. Add cottage cheese, shredded carrots, celery, marshmallows, radishes, orange slices or whatever you happen to have on hand. Put it back in the fridge until it's firm, and serve.

☛ **Flapper Pie**. A good pie for times when fruit is scarce. And it's delicious, too!

Pie Crust:
1½ cups (375 mL) graham wafer crumbs
1 Tbsp. (15 mL) sugar
⅓ cup (75 mL) melted butter

Mix, then press in pie plate and bake at 350°F (180°C) for 10 minutes.

Filling:
2 cups (450 mL) milk
2 egg yolks
⅓ cup (75 mL) sugar
3 Tbsp. (50 mL) corn starch
Pinch of salt
1 Tbsp. (15 mL) butter
1 tsp. (5 mL) vanilla

Heat 1½ cups (375 mL) of the milk in double boiler. Combine the egg yolks, sugar, corn starch, salt and the remainder of the milk. Add this mixture to the hot milk, cook until thick. Remove from heat, and add butter and vanilla. Cool slightly, and pour into pie crust.

Meringue:
2 egg whites
2 Tbsp. (30 mL) cold water
4 Tbsp. (60 mL) sugar
Pinch of cream of tartar

Whip together egg whites, water, cream of tartar, and then add sugar. Spread the meringue on top of the pie filling and bake at 350°F (180°C) until golden brown, about 10–15 minutes.

The Powwow

A Native tradition, a powwow is a gathering of Native, Métis and non-Native people to dance, sing, socialize and generally have a good time. Powwows can last as long as a week or just for an afternoon, but they often take place over a weekend, with the grand entry of elders, dignitaries and dancers happening on Friday night.

In the wee hours of Sunday morning, the last competition—men's traditional dance—closes out the festivities. Dances include fancy-dance, traditional, jingle dance and grass dance in all the age categories, right down to "Tiny Tots." Drummers come from near and far. Beadwork, ribbon shirts and handmade jewellery are on display—and the food is plentiful: Native tacos, meatball soup, and of course, bannock...

☛ Bannock

In a large bowl, combine:
6 cups (1.4 L) flour
2 Tbsp. (30 mL) baking powder
1 tsp. (5 mL) salt
1 tsp. (5 mL) sugar
Make a hollow in the dry ingredients, then add:
2 cups (450 mL) water
6 Tbsp. (100 mL) oil
Mix well. Knead the dough until soft and only slightly sticky.
Let dough sit for 15 minutes, then roll onto a lightly floured
cookie sheet. Pierce the surface of the dough with a fork in several places, then bake at 350°F (180°C) for about 15 minutes
until golden brown. Cut into squares and serve.

The Come and Go Tea

To celebrate a milestone anniversary or an important birthday,
a "Come and Go" tea is *de rigeur*. A hall is rented, and friends
and family of the honoured guests provide the refreshments,
which might include:

☛ **Matrimonial Cake.** No one knows why the confection
known as "date squares" almost everywhere else in the
country is called "matrimonial cake" in Saskatchewan,
but it is. Here's the recipe:

Date Filling:
1 package dates
1 cup (250 mL) sugar
1 cup (250 mL) water

Boil together all ingredients until thickened.

Base:
¾ cup (175 mL) brown sugar
1½ cups (375 mL) oatmeal
1 cup (250 mL) flour
1 tsp. (5 mL) baking soda
½ cup (125 mL) butter
¼ tsp. (1 mL) salt

Mix ingredients together well. Put three-quarters of the mixture into a baking pan, then add a layer of date filling. Sprinkle the remainder of the mixture on top. Bake at 350°F (180°C) until golden brown.

Coffee Row

Definition: a bunch of people going to a small-town restaurant for coffee; usually segregated by gender, with men's and women's coffee rows happening at different times of the morning. Groups are sometimes also separated into early riser groups and those who like to sleep in. If the restauranteur is a lazy type, he or she gives the key to a trusted customer, who will open up the joint and brew the first pot of coffee!

4-H Achievement Day

An organization for young people aged 6–21, the 4-H has been active in Saskatchewan for 90 years and still runs 231 clubs with over 4000 members. Kids can try their hand at woodworking, gardening, sewing, public speaking, and the latest addition, dog clubs—but the most popular clubs in Saskatchewan remain the livestock ones. Each year 4-H members hold an "Achievement Day" in their community to display their projects. And in case you were wondering, the four "Hs" are "Heart, Head, Hands and Health."

The Smoker

A smoker—as in "There's a smoker at the Legion tomorrow"—is a gathering with conversation and alcoholic refreshments, used as a fundraiser for a community group. The door prizes are sometimes euphemistically listed as "Third Prize: hockey puck; Second Prize: hockey puck; First Prize: *Texas* hockey puck."

Wedding Fun

For many years, newlyweds could expect their neighbours to "chivaree" them on their wedding night. Friends and family would surround the honeymooners' house and make as much racket, commotion and hullaballoo as possible by yelling, playing musical instruments or banging on pots and pans. The chivaree-ers wouldn't leave until the couple made an appearance—at which time teasing was in order. The couple could shoo away the intruders or invite them in for a drink, but when the party was over, it was over, and the bride and groom could retire in peace.

 DID YOU KNOW?

Another vanished Saskatchewan custom was the "mock wedding," in which a cross-dressed pair of actors put on a play to celebrate a wedding or anniversary. The laughs came mainly when big beefy farmers and ranchers played their feminine roles to the hilt.

The Homemakers Meeting

At the turn of the century, small women's groups such as the "Prosperity Homemakers' Society" and the "Open Door Circle" of Mair provided social outings and an opportunity to discuss problems faced by women on the prairie. In 1911, various organizations united as the "Homemakers," and clubs spread rapidly throughout the province.

Homemaker clubs were non-partisan and non-sectarian, and they offered a welcome to women new to a community—particularly after World War II, when many war brides and refugees came to the province. The clubs worked for the community as well, setting up clinics or raising money for local causes. They put on art exhibits, held handicraft fairs and compiled community histories. And "Homemakers Cookbooks" are the gold standard in many a Saskatchewan home!

Telemiracle

In 1977 the Kinsmen began "Telemiracle," a 20-hour telethon to raise funds for people with special needs. It was so successful that it's now an annual event and has raised more than $68 million. Telemiracle regularly sets records for per-capita giving: It now raises over $3 million annually. Notable guests have included Theresa Sokyrka, the Barra-McNeils, Bob McGrath of *Sesame Street,* Alan Thicke, The Irish Rovers, Michelle Wright and many others.

FOOD, DRINK AND FUN

Western Delicacies

For an entire year, CBC's Amy Jo Ehman and her husband decided to eat nothing but foods produced in Saskatchewan. They feasted on traditional Skatchie food such as pike (and other lake fish), white-tailed deer steaks, moose soup, wild rice, stewed rhubarb, crabapple and chokecherry jelly, lingonberry jam and Saskatoon pie—as well as a lot of more exotic fare from the province's wide variety of ethnic groups.

And Finish Off with a Brew or Two

Beeradvocate magazine lists 23 brewpubs, two breweries, two beer bars, and one homebrew shop under "Saskatchewan." Best-known Saskatchewan beers include Molson's "Bohemian" (recently made available in Ontario, too) and "Pilsner," which have been brewed since 1926. Saskatoon's Great Western Brewing Company also brews a line of products and won a bronze medal for their Western Premium Light beer in the World Beer Cup.

Roadside Art

When huge, round hay bales began replacing their smaller rect-angular cousins several years ago, it didn't take long for Saskatchewanians to find a way to have a little fun with the new format. Sometimes a wag will stick a pair of pants and some boots out of the end of a bale that's near the highway—to make it look as though the farmer is trapped inside. And a similar sense of humour has led to the creation of several "Boot Hills." Not the Wild West cemetery kind, but fences that have been decorated with dozens of cast-off shoes!

EDUCATION STATS

*From the one-room schoolhouse to advanced university facilities,
Skatchies have always been fans of book-learnin'. Read on!
(And don't worry, there won't be a pop quiz at the end.)*

Crunching the Numbers

Based on the most recent census data, here's how educated
Saskatchewanians aged 25–64 are:

Level Completed	Number	Percent of Population
Less than high school	134,585	28.3
High school	103,875	21.8
Trades	76,050	16.0
College	74,407	15.6
University	87,005	18.3

Trendy Women

The same census also reveals a
Skatchie trend: a 21-percent increase in
graduates from post-secondary schools.
College-level graduates had the largest
increase, with women making up
64 percent of the growth. University
grads were the next largest, with
women accounting for a whopping
72 percent of the increase. A larger
proportion of women than men
in Saskatchewan now has a
university degree.

Education Everywhere

Saskatchewan has two universities, eight regional colleges, and a college with four urban campuses:

- Carlton Trail Regional College
- Cumberland Regional College
- North East Regional College
- Northlands Regional College
- North West Regional College
- Parkland Regional College
- Prairie West Regional College
- Southeast Regional College
- Saskatchewan Institute of Applied Science and Technology, with campuses in Regina, Moose Jaw, Saskatoon and Prince Albert
- The University of Saskatchewan
- The University of Regina

Higher Power Education

Saskatchewan currently has 15 post-secondary religious institutions. More bible schools and colleges have been started in Saskatchewan than in any other province or territory.

EDUCATIONAL INNOVATIONS

The Barter System at Its Finest

In 1969 and 1970, the University of Saskatchewan offered a grain-for-fees program. Children of farmers could deliver up to $300 worth of barley, oats or wheat to help cover the cost of tuition.

Buffy, Networking

Buffy Sainte-Marie, internationally adored Saskatchewan musician, holds degrees in education, oriental philosophy, and a PhD in fine art. She's currently spearheading the Cradleboard Teaching Project, which, among other things, builds computer networking relationships between Native and non-Native schools. The pilot project involved schools from Hawaii and Saskatchewan.

Reading and 'Riting and 'Rithmetic

Saskatchewan's first schools were one-room schoolhouses. Small school divisions were formed, and the Dominion government ordered that Sections 11 and 29 of every township be deemed school sections—and by the 1930s nearly 5000 one-room schools were in operation. The basic schoolroom had a blackboard, some shelves, a teacher's desk, single or double desks for students and a pot-bellied stove.

Outbuildings included two privies, a stable and sometimes a teacherage. The average school had about 15 students, in grades six to eight, who arrived by foot, wagon or horseback. Schools were used for community events, such as dances—and the annual Christmas concert was always a district highlight. Improved transportation and the disappearance of small farms brought the era of the one-room school to a close.

First in the World

In 1976, classes began at the Saskatchewan Indian Federated College, a University of Regina affiliate. It became known as "the Indian Oxford," because it was the first school of higher education in the world controlled by indigenous people. In 2003 the college moved into new digs on the University of Regina campus and got a new name: The First Nations University of Canada.

Monk-y Business

St. Peter's Abbey near Muenster was Canada's first Benedictine abbey. In 1921 the monks founded St. Peter's College, which for many years was one of the largest educational institutions in the West.

Don't Send "Little House on the Prairie"

In the 1890s, the wife of the Governor General founded the "Lady Aberdeen Association for the Distribution of Literature to Settlers in the West." Known as the "Aberdeen Association," it provided much-needed reading fodder for isolated Saskatchewan homesteaders, and the association eventually evolved into the largest, free circulating library in Canada.

"Highways to Adventure"

As early as 1931, Saskatchewan's correspondence school experimented with using radio to supplement course material, but it wasn't until 1941 that the Department of Education began offering regular radio programming. The first programs were a language arts series and a music hour. Later, national school broadcasts were added to the schedule.

Shawking!

Renowned British playwright and wit George Bernard Shaw once said that the University of Saskatchewan was "apparently half a century ahead of Cambridge in Science, and of Oxford in common sense."

DID YOU KNOW?

The University of Saskatchewan established the first scholarship in Canada to fund students of gay, lesbian and bisexual studies. The Peter Millard Scholarship Fund's inaugural year was 1995.

Train-ing Farmers

From 1914 to 1922, the "Better Farming Train" travelled the province, bringing information about the latest agricultural methods to farm families. The train had 14–16 cars, including a "nursery coach" that provided child care; several cars filled with exhibits of livestock, machinery and crops; and three lecture coaches—one of which offered demonstrations of "domestic science" for farm wives.

Not Liquored Up

In 1932, the Bronfman family came to the University of Saskatchewan with an offer to build a state-of-the-art sports complex, complete with football field, baseball diamond, swimming pool and curling rink. James S. ("Butch") Thompson—president of the university and a Presbyterian minister—decided that there would be "no booze on this campus" and turned down the offer. The Bronfmans went on to become one of McGill University's biggest donors.

STELLAR STUDENTS AND EXTRAORDINARY EDUCATORS

One of Sylvia's Firsts

Sylvia Fedoruk—medical researcher, award-winning athlete and Saskatchewan's first female lieutenant-governor—was also the first woman to serve as chancellor of the University of Saskatchewan, from 1986 to 1991.

Teacher, Teacher

Saskatchewan's first trained teacher was Onesime Dorval, who taught in the Battleford and Batoche regions from 1877 to 1914.

Try, Try Again

Lydia Gruchy graduated at the top of her class in theological college and went to Kamsack to work as a lay minister. She first applied for ordination as a United Church minister in 1926. When she was turned down, she reapplied every two years until she was finally ordained in 1936. She was the first woman in Canada to receive an honorary Doctor of Divinity degree.

Geology Genius

Bill Serjeant of Saskatoon not only wrote a 10-volume history of geology and geologists, but he also had the world's largest private collection on the history of geology and an 85,000-volume personal library! Serjeant was also a harmonica player, a collector, naturalist and author of more than 50 articles about Sherlock Holmes.

Where's the Beef?

Hilda Neatby, a Saskatoon history professor, was the only woman on the Massey Commission, which reviewed learning and culture in Canada. In 1953 Neatby wrote a scathing analysis of the country's educational systems called *So Little for the Mind.* The book stirred up controversy and became a surprise best-seller.

Sit-In

In 1971, students at the University of Saskatchewan occupied the eighth floor of the Arts building to protest the replacement of economics professor John Richards. Students felt that Richards—member of the NDP Waffle and a political candidate—was being punished for his political activity. As many as 1500 students at a time took part in the protest.

"C": Like a Cookie with a Bite Out of It

Anna Ingham, who began her teaching career in a one-room school in Yorkton, caused a stir among Saskatchewan educators. By the end of each school year, her grade one students were reading far above their grade level. Soon teachers were making pilgrimages from all over the province to see how she did it. "You can teach children anything if you put it in a story that's real in their lives," she said. In 1967, Ingham published *The Blended Sound-Sight Method of Learning,* a bible for elementary teachers ever since.

HEALTH FACTS AND FIRSTS

Saskatchewan was the first jurisdiction in North America to introduce universal health care. Despite initial skepticism from many quarters, the idea proved to be such a good one that it wasn't long before the rest of Canada followed suit—and today, "medicare" is one of the things that defines our country. Saskatchewan continues to develop new programs—and some of the best health care professionals in the world call the province home.

Dead Average

Life expectancy in Saskatchewan is 78.3 years—exactly the same as the national average life expectancy.

Room for Improvement

Skatchies could probably raise their life expectancy by improving their record on two health issues: The province's smokers make up 18.7 percent of the population (Canadian average is 16.5 percent), and Saskatchewan comes in fourth in province-by-province rankings of obesity among adults.

Raising the Flag

The first Red Cross emblem ever used in Canada was attached to a horse-drawn wagon of a volunteer ambulance brigade, on the battlefield at Batoche.

Stone Cold Miracle

At 2:30 AM on February 23, 1994, two-year-old Karlee Kosolofski toddled out the door after her father as he left for work. She was wearing her pyjamas, and the temperature in Rouleau that night plummeted to -22°C. By the time the tyke was discovered missing, nearly six hours later, her little body was almost frozen solid. Karlee's left leg had to be amputated, and she had to undergo some surgeries and skin grafts—but to everyone's amazement, she survived. Karlee made it into the *Guinness Book of World Records* for surviving the lowest body temperature ever recorded: 14.16°C.

Groovy, Man

The word "psychedelic" was coined in 1957 in Weyburn by psychiatrist Humphrey Osmond. Osmond and Dr. Abram Hoffer were experimenting with LSD as a way to treat alcoholism. During the latter half of the 1950s, the two doctors treated almost 2000 alcoholics and managed a "cure" rate of 40–45 percent. Osmond later turned his friend, novelist Aldous Huxley, on to mescaline. Huxley wrote about his hallucinogenic experiences in *The Doors of Perception,* required reading for '60s hippies and the source for the name of the rock group The Doors.

Lifesaver

Dr. James Till of Lloydminster was a pioneer of stem cell research. The findings of Till and his fellow researcher Dr. Ernest McCulloch led to the development of bone marrow transplant treatment for certain types of cancer. When Till started working at the Ontario Cancer Institute in 1958, the survival rate for leukemia was 50 percent. Today it's greater than 80 percent.

Leading the Way

In 1947, Saskatchewan became the first province to offer universal hospital insurance for its residents. Annual fees were $5 per person, or $30 per family.

DID YOU  KNOW?

In 1914, the Rural Municipality of Sarnia (in the Holdfast area) agreed to pay its doctor because locals couldn't afford health care. It was the first time in North America that a community had hired a doctor.

Nursing Back to Health

Doctor shortages in rural Saskatchewan are being eased by a program designed to put nurse practitioners into doctor-challenged areas. Nurse practitioners—registered nurses who've completed two extra years of training—diagnose, prescribe medication and work in concert with other health care professionals. The pilot project took place in 1995 in the Beechy-Kyle area, where Dr. Tony Hamilton had been looking after 3500 patients.

But No One Could Read the Picket Signs

July 1, 1962, was the date set for the implementation of Saskatchewan's Medical Care Act, with its universal government-funded insurance program. The College of Physicians and Surgeons, backed by the American Medical Association, opposed "socialized medicine" and warned of a mass exodus of doctors. But Premier Woodrow Lloyd held firm, and on July 1 the vast majority of the province's doctors went on strike. An influx of medicos from other parts of Canada and from Britain and the U.S. arrived to provide care, and the strike ended after three weeks. Some doctors left the province, but many others were recruited to come to Saskatchewan, and applications to the University of Saskatchewan's medical school skyrocketed. Three years later, the Hall Report recommended that Canada implement a national plan, modelled on Saskatchewan's success.

HEALERS

Bethune's Left-Hand Woman

Jean Ewen of Harris and Saskatoon graduated from nursing school at the beginning of the Great Depression and joined a Franciscan mission to China. Ewen quickly picked up Mandarin and plunged into her work in the politically volatile country. After several years she returned home but was soon hired by the famous Dr. Norman Bethune to accompany him to China in 1938.

With the Sino-Japanese war raging, Bethune and Ewen faced incredible obstacles and narrowly escaped death more than once. Each was as stubborn and passionate as the other, however, and after one argument, Bethune abandoned Ewen at a Red Cross Hospital. She continued her work in China until 1939, when she returned to Canada and married a veteran of the Spanish Civil War. After her death in 1987, Ewen's family spread her ashes in northern China's "Revolutionary Martyrs' Cemetery."

Top Doc

Dr. Ali Rajput of Saskatoon has followed more patients with Parkinson's disease than any other doctor in the world and is an international authority on the diagnosis and treatment of the illness. He's also the first Muslim Canadian to have received the Order of Canada (1997).

Death Toll

The Spanish influenza pandemic of 1918 hit Saskatchewan hard, with one in four families infected. There was a shortage of doctors in the province—about 10 percent of them were on military service and many more had contracted the influenza themselves. And 87 percent of the population lived in rural areas, where doctors were scarcest. Fifty thousand people in Canada died during the epidemic—5000 of them in Saskatchewan.

And the Winner Is...Me

Founder of the Aboriginal Nurses Association of Canada and a life-long champion of public health services for Aboriginal people, nurse Jean Goodwill received many awards in her lifetime. In 1981 she received the Jean Goodwill Award, which had been created in her honour by the Manitoba Indian Nurses Association.

Medical Visionary

Dr. David Baltzan, who grew up in the Lipton area, had a 50-year medical career in Saskatoon. He was one of the first doctors to posit a link between smoking and heart disease, and he was a pioneer in the field of transplants.

Cracking Good Story

May Tuplin saved her pennies for 10 years in order to go to Chicago to study to become a chiropractor. She graduated in 1923 and practised in the Beechy area for over half a century, until she was well into her 80s.

Saddlebag Surgeon

Dr. Murrough O'Brien was born in Delhi, India, in 1868. He flunked out of medical school in London, bet his last five pounds on a racehorse and won enough money to emigrate to Canada. After graduating from medical school in Canada, O'Brien worked as a country doctor, first in Manitoba and then in Saskatchewan.

He rode his horse through downpours and blizzards and faced every sort of disease and injury, performing tonsillectomies and appendectomies—and delivering more than 9000 babies before he lost count! In 1954, at the age of 86, O'Brien—still practising medicine—received an honour from the Saskatchewan government: An island and a bay in the Lac La Ronge area were given his name.

Doctor Duo

Doctors C.J. and Sigga Houston set up a practice in Yorkton in the 1920s. C.J. worked as a general practitioner, and because a female doctor was a relative novelty at the time, Sigga began specializing in treating children and pregnant women. When the Depression hit, patients paid their fees in whatever they could spare: a bit of meat, a cord of wood or a buffalo coat. Before her death at the age of 102 in 1996, Sigga was celebrated as Canada's oldest living female doctor.

LOOK WHAT I FOUND!

You name it, Saskatchewan's scientists and inventors have found it, imagined it, designed it or built it!

Long Time Gone

The oldest fossils found in Saskatchewan are 1,700,000,000-year-old microscopic cells of blue algae known as stromatolites.

Crocodile Rock

"Bert," the fossil of a 92,000,000-year-old type of crocodile—a *Teleorhinus*—was discovered in the Carrot River area in 1991.

T-Rex

In 1994, "Scotty," the fossil of a 65,000,000-year-old *Tyrannosaurus Rex*, was found near Eastend. The skeleton is about 65 percent complete and ranks among the top specimens in the world.

Poop Happens

Scientists discovered some dinosaur dung the following year, again near Eastend. The single carnivore "coprolite" was the largest ever found. It contained pieces of undigested bone and weighed almost 7 kilograms!

Eyes on the Skies

Amateur astronomer Vince Pietriw of Regina discovered a new comet in 2001. The comet appears in the summer sky every five years and is officially known as "Comet Pietriw." Vince says finding the comet was "like winning the 6/49."

Extra-Terrestrial

A couple of decades ago, Melvin Christensen of Kyle found a funny-looking rock while he was cultivating a field. Recently, scientists from Calgary and Washington identified the magnetic, nickel-based specimen as a 7-kilogram meteorite.

Just before a meteorite enters the earth's atmosphere, it's travelling 71 kilometres per second—or about 2500 times faster than a fast baseball pitch.

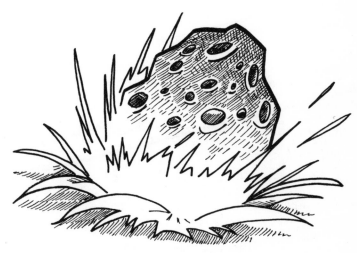

INVENTIONS

Blowtorch

Bill McIntyre of Swift Current built a life-sized mechanical horse in 1952. "Blowtorch" toured North America, was exhibited at Madison Square Garden and was featured in *Time* magazine. Blowtorch also delighted audiences at the Saskatchewan pavilion at Expo in Vancouver in 1986.

"Make-Do's"

Skatchie farmers are infamous for putting together whatever they need with whatever they've got lying around. Some of the most creative include:

☛ A bull-powered, treadmill-based milking machine, circa 1933

☛ A dog-powered water pump, 1940

☛ A wind-powered car, 1972

DID YOU KNOW?

Douglas Hougen of Sceptre invented the Rotabroach Cutter, a spot-weld cutter able to slice cleanly through heavy-gauge metal.

Keep on Truckin'

Art Bergan and a team of researchers in Saskatoon developed a weigh scale that weighs vehicles in motion, up to 70 kilometres per hour.

SCIENTISTS OF NOTE

Nobel Winners: Better Living Through Chemistry

☛ Dr. Gerhard Herzberg, who worked at the University of Saskatchewan for a decade in the '30s and '40s, was the first Canadian to win the Nobel Prize for Chemistry (1971). His field was the study of atomic and molecular spectroscopy.

☛ Henry Taube of Neudorf won the 1983 Nobel Prize for Chemistry for his work with dissolved organic solids. He also won the Linus Pauling Award. Dr. Taube said, "Science as an intellectual exercise enriches our culture and is in itself ennobling."

Big Wheeler

Rosthern-area farmer Seager Wheeler practically invented farming on the prairie. He developed new machinery, wrote about agricultural subjects and, starting in 1911, won *five* world wheat championships, a record that has never been equalled. The three strains of wheat he developed are Marquis 10B, Red Bobs, and Kitchener.

It IS Rocket Science!

The first Canadian experiment aboard a space shuttle was designed by University of Saskatchewan professor Louis Delbaere. The Discovery shuttle conducted Delbaere's experiment about crystallization in space in 1990.

And Dr. Henry Thode, born near Dundurn, is the only Canadian scientist to receive and study specimens of the moon (brought back to earth by Apollo 17 astronauts).

Cancer Research…and Sylvia Again

And in 1951, a team of researchers—including future Lieutenant-Governor Sylvia Fedoruk—designed the Cobalt-60 and began using cobalt radiation to treat cancer patients. Their first patient, a 43-year-old mother of four, beat her cancer and went on to live for another 50 years! Fedoruk later developed the Dosimeter, which helped to regulate radiation dosages, and a device to test for thyroid cancer.

Particle-larly Smart

University of Saskatchewan particle physicist Chary Rangacharyulu helped to discover a new subatomic particle. The find came in ninth on *Discovery* magazine's 2003 list of the "Top 100 Science Stories."

Stringing Us Along

Robert Moody of Saskatoon co-discovered the Kac-Moody algebras, the basic mathematical structure that underlies superstring theory.

Sweet!

In the 1950s, Raymond Lemieux of the University of Saskatchewan was the first chemist to produce table sugar by synthetic means. The discovery led to many others, including understanding how proteins bind to sugar receptors on blood cells.

Cream of the Crop

Marianna Foldvaria, a University of Saskatchewan scientist, has developed "Biphasix," which could help take the place of needles for some patients. An insulin patch and a cream to treat human papilloma virus (HPV) are expected to be on the market within the next few years.

Because Rust Never Sleeps

Margaret Newton, one of the first women in the country to study agriculture at university, became the leading Canadian authority on cereal rusts in the 1920s.

In 1992, University of Saskatchewan soil scientist Jeff Schoenau developed a Band-Aid-like plastic resin strip to analyze soil fertility. Since its inception, the technology has helped to improve yields on 3.4 million acres of farmland throughout western Canada.

Lots of Hype

In the 1930s, University of Saskatchewan professor J.S. Fulton came up with one of the first vaccines against equine encephalomyelitis. And veterinarian Stephen Acres developed the first vaccine against calf scours.

Not Found at Timmy's

Professor Akira Hirose of the University of Saskatchewan's Department of Physics constructed Canada's first "tokamak"— a doughnut-shaped fusion device.

SCIENCE PROJECTS

Trip the Light Fantastic

Canada's biggest scientific project in a generation, the Canadian Light Source Synchotron (CLS), opened in Saskatoon in October 2004. The size of a football field, the $175 million CLS uses "wigglers" and "undulators" to produce more light from electron streams, which allows matter to be seen at the atomic level. The synchrotron has applications from cancer research to manufacturing microscopic machines to creating stronger metal alloys for space travel. About a dozen different countries involving 140 scientists work at the CLS.

In the Vanguard of the Digital Revolution

Crown Corporation SaskTel was the first company to develop and operate a large-scale fibre optic network in the early 1980s. When the company started building the network, the longest one in the world was 10 kilometres. The Sask Tel network covered 3268 kilometres!

Environmental Detectives

A new facility at the University of Regina will help to study trace amounts of pollutants. The research team will focus on very small amounts of pesticides in Saskatchewan's ecosystems.

Immunization Record

The federal government recently announced a $25-million contribution towards an international vaccine centre in Saskatoon. Experts in human health, vet medicine and agriculture plan to work together to research diseases such as hepatitis C, West Nile virus and severe acute respiratory syndrome (SARS).

Good Things Come in Small Packages

At the University of Regina, a powerful computer the size of a small filing cabinet is being used to research subatomic matter. The nucleus of an atom is made up of protons and neutrons, which themselves are made up of quarks and gluons. But what are quarks and gluons made of? The answer may come from Regina....

Just the Tip of the Iceberg

A University of Regina research team led by Roy Cullamore studied microbial communities living on parts of the wreck of the ship *Titanic*. The team's goal is to develop treatments for contaminated water.

Eco-Town

Craik, a village in south-central Saskatchewan with a population of about 400, aims to be a leader in environmentally friendly living. The Craik Sustainable Living Project Eco-Centre is a multi-purpose facility that has become a focal point for educational programming on sustainability.

The building was designed to use as few energy requirements as possible. It was constructed with timbers from grain elevators in Craik and Maymont that were slated for demolition, with durum wheat straw bales and with 3000 bricks recycled from a torn-down school. The facility also features solar heating, an earth-tube fresh air system, an in-house biological water treatment system and a composting toilet septic system. Plans are now underway for a new housing development that will be populated by several families living sustainably.

THE STATS

With high average incomes, low housing costs and every kind of amenity, Saskatchewan has been named one of the best places in the world to live. And although the province is well known for its wheat fields, you may be surprised by the variety of money-making ventures in Saskatchewan…

The Bottom Line

Latest statistics peg Saskatchewan's Gross Domestic Product (GDP) at $36,519 billion, or about 3 percent of the Canadian economy. Of that GDP, 8.7 percent was derived from agriculture, 12.3 percent from other primary industries, 12 percent from manufacturing or construction and a whopping 67 percent came from the service sector.

Royal Treasury

Saskatchewan's Crown Corporations account for 15 percent of the province's GDP.

Resource-ful

About 95 percent of all goods produced in the province depend directly on resources: grain, livestock, oil and gas, potash, uranium and wood, along with their refined products. The largest single export commodity is crude oil.

Not Too Taxing

Saskatchewan's provincial sales tax is 5 percent—the lowest of any province that charges a sales tax. People on the Skatchie side of Lloydminster get some exemptions so as to keep them in synch with the Alberta half of the city—which, of course, has no sales tax.

In the House

Regina is tied for number one on a list that ranks the world's cities for affordable home ownership. People in the Queen City, along with those in Fort Wayne, Indiana and Youngstown, Ohio, won't have to save long to buy a house. Saskatoon came in at number 15.

Show Me the Money

The average per-capita annual income in the province is $34,700. That's less than the national average, but more than three times the global average.

Pogey

Saskatchewan's current rate of unemployment is 5.1 percent, less than the national rate, which came in at 6.2 percent.

Saskatchewan has the highest rate of volunteerism in Canada. Every year, 323,000 citizens volunteer 49.7 million hours. That's the equivalent of 26,000 full-time jobs!

AGRICULTURE

Long Way to the Nearest Elevator

In 1754, grain was grown in the Carrot River Valley region of what would one day become Saskatchewan—151 years later.

Homesteading

The Dominion Lands Act of 1872 encouraged the settlement of the Prairies by selling 160 acres for $10 to any farmer who agreed to cultivate at least 40 acres and to build a permanent dwelling within three years. In a twist unique to Canada, there was also provision for a farmer to buy a neighbouring homestead, an important point for those who settled in the arid Palliser triangle. About 478,000 square kilometres of land was granted under the Act.

The Dirty Thirties

- At the start of the Great Depression, Saskatchewan was the fourth wealthiest province in Canada, and the average person in the province had one of the greatest net cash incomes in the world. After consecutive years of grasshoppers, hail and dust, the province plummeted to last place.

- By 1932, 66 percent of the rural population was on relief.

- The price of wheat fell to 35¢ per bushel in 1932, down from $1.60 per bushel in 1929.

- In 1937, wheat production fell to 2.5 bushels per acre, from an average of 25–30 bushels per acre during the 1920s.

- Once completely self-sufficient in animal feed, the province had to import feed from Alberta and Manitoba.

- Between 1931 and 1941, 250,000 people left the prairie provinces.

☛ Gasoline became too expensive, so cars were hitched to horses.

☛ In 1931–32, almost 10,000 homeless, unemployed men passed through Saskatchewan Relief Commission work camps.

☛ Governments struggled to deal with the situation, but ordinary Canadians pitched in to help—Winnipeg Boy Scouts and Girl Guides collected clothing; eastern provinces sent salt cod, canned milk and turnips; and canned goods arrived from Ontario.

Record-Breaking Ag News

☛ Saskatchewan produces 10 percent of the world's wheat.

☛ Saskatchewan is the world's lead exporter of lentils, mustard, and canary seed.

☛ The Crop Development Centre in Saskatoon is the largest plant-breeding operation in the world.

☛ Of all the wheat grown in Canada, 54 percent comes from Saskatchewan.

☛ Saskatchewan has 28.8 percent of crop sales in Canada, giving it the largest share of total cash receipts.

☛ Saskatchewan has 773 farms producing certified organic products. Half of Canada's organic field crops come from the province, and 1.5 percent of all Saskatchewan farms report some organic production.

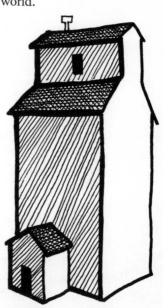

Berry Interesting

Last Mountain Berry Farm of Southey is the largest processor of saskatoon berries in Canada—and probably the world.

Top Crops
The province's three major crops are wheat, canola and barley.

DID YOU  KNOW?

In 1929 a Plymouth Rock pullet named "Lady Victorine" laid 358 eggs in 365 days, a world record. She was owned by the University of Saskatchewan.

Psst! Wanna Buy Some Durum?
Rock-bottom grain prices in the 1930s led some erstwhile respectable farmers in the Val Marie area into a life of crime. When they found that American elevator agents were paying 10¢ more than local ones, the farmers started smuggling wagon-loads of grain across the border.

Git Along Little Dogies

In 1898, Moose Jaw–area rancher George Tuxford led a herd of cattle from his farm across the Canadian Rockies to Dawson City. It was the longest cattle drive in Canadian history.

Grand Old Man of Canadian Agriculture

William Motherwell pioneered dry-land farming techniques, helped found the Territorial Grain Growers' Association, served as Saskatchewan's first minister of agriculture and as federal agriculture minister, too. He left politics when he turned 80, saying, "When a man drops out at the age of 80, people can't say he's a quitter." Motherwell's homestead near Abernethy, with its two-storey stone house, has been restored to the 1910–14 period.

Support System

The Saskatchewan Abilities Council has a "Farmers with Disabilities" program. Neale Abrey, a quadriplegic farmer from Simpson, helped to establish it in June 1986.

Restaurant on Wheels

In the '20s, it was common for "cook cars" to travel with custom threshing crews. Two women usually ran the cook car, which had a coal and wood stove but no refrigeration. They got up before dawn to start breakfast, and by the time they'd finished the supper dishes and set the table for the morning, it was often near midnight. The cooks made three large meals a day, complete with pies, homemade bread, cakes and doughnuts… and were paid about 40¢ an hour. Persistent flies were a problem for the cooks—and sometimes so were persistent threshers!

Out to Pasture

There are 60 federal and 56 provincial community pastures in Saskatchewan, covering 2.57 million acres. They're used mainly for grazing cattle.

OTHER INDUSTRIES

We've Got Lots of That

Where better to build one of the largest wheat-fed ethanol plants in North America than in Lloydminster, on the Saskatchewan/Alberta border? The new Husky plant is expected to produce 130 million litres of fuel per year.

Got Even More of That
The Centennial Wind Power Project near Swift Current operates 83 wind turbines, which generate enough energy to service 64,000 homes.

The largest potash mine in the world is the IMC mine near Esterhazy. And Saskatchewan is the world's largest exporter of potash—it has an estimated 75 percent of the world's supply of the mineral. The province's potash deposits were originally discovered by men drilling for oil.

Glow in the Dark

The province is also the world's largest supplier of uranium, with 30 percent of the global supply. Saskatchewan is the only producer of uranium in Canada and mines the highest-grade deposit in the world, at McArthur River. Saskatchewan contributed uranium to the Manhattan Project, which produced the bombs that were dropped on Hiroshima and Nagasaki.

Ach Der Lieber!
Saskatchewan's forestry industry is based on woodlands the size of the country of Germany. Twenty-three percent of the province's land mass is covered by commercial forest.

Banded Trees

The Meadow Lake Tribal Council owns NorSask Forest Products Inc., one of the province's largest companies. It's also the largest Aboriginal-owned forest products company in Canada.

Novel Pulp

The Millar Western pulp mill in northern Saskatchewan uses a chlorine-free process that requires half as many trees as the low-yield process. It's also the world's first successful zero liquid effluent discharge pulp mill.

DID YOU  KNOW?

Saskatchewan has Canada's second-largest energy reserves. (Alberta has the largest.)

A Girl's Best Friend

The province is home to a large area of kimberlite fields, which often produce diamonds. Exploration is underway....

Brainwaves

Some wacky manufacturing ideas have popped up in the province in recent years. "Spudco," a potato farming and french fry–making operation near Lucky Lake, lost millions of dollars for investors and taxpayers, and a Meadow Lake plan to supply 1.56 billion chopsticks per year to Japan never got off the ground. Other ideas that didn't quite come to fruition include a plastic shopping-cart factory and a scheme to ship pet gophers to Asia.

No More Rubbernecking

SaskTel was the first telecommunications company in Canada to eliminate party lines in rural areas.

Another Brick in the Wall

The Claybank Brick Plant near Avonlea opened in 1914 and produced brick that graced the façade of the Chateau Frontenac in Québec City, brick that lined the fire boxes of CN and CPR locomotives, and even brick that was used in the construction of the rocket launch pads at Cape Canaveral. The plant has been preserved and allows visitors to follow the entire brick-making process. It's designated as a National Historic Site.

Remove the Oil But Not the Soil

A Regina company has figured out a way to clean up contaminated sites (such as gas stations or oil refineries) by developing more than 70 new technologies. Ground Effects Environmental Services does business all over the world.

Not Just Good for You, Essential

Saskatchewan's Bioriginal Food & Science Corporation is the world's top supplier of essential fatty acids—the omega-3 or omega-6 products you see at grocery or health-food stores. The company extracts the oils from Saskatchewan-grown flax and borage.

CO-OPS

Co-operates with Others

Nobody does co-ops better than Saskatchewan. There are currently 1306 co-operatives in the province, generating $7 billion in revenue. The first one was the Harmony Co-operative Industrial Association—a co-operative farm established by about 50 idealistic people near Tantallon in 1895.

Lots of Co-operation

Federated Co-operatives Ltd. of Saskatoon is Canada's largest co-operative, based on net income.

DID YOU  KNOW?

North America's first co-operative oil refinery opened in 1935 in Regina.

Even Cows Co-operate

Between 1897 and 1905, 14 co-operative creameries were established in the province.

Jump Right In

Ed Partridge and W.R. Motherwell led the fight for two farmer-owned co-operatives that would revolutionize the grain trade: the United Grain Growers and the Saskatchewan Wheat Pool. The Wheat Pool is now Canada's largest publicly traded agricultural co-operative.

Top of the World, Ma

A co-operative elevator in Cabri set a world elevator record by handling 600,000 bushels of grain in 1916.

Northern Co-operators

The first northern co-operative was a fishers' co-op at Kinoosao, Reindeer Lake, in 1945.

Even Cold Hard Cash Co-operates

The Saskatchewan Co-operative Credit Society (now Credit Union Central) was English-Canada's first central credit union system.

Co-op Farms

Although farmers are often portrayed as rugged individualists, Saskatchewan was once home to 32 co-operative farms. The CCF government initiated the idea in the 1940s to give returning veterans a start in farming. The largest and most persistent was the Matador Co-op Farm, created on land broken out of the old Matador Community Pasture between Kyle and Beechy. A smaller version of the farm operates now as the Matador Farming Pool Limited and is home to eight farmers and their families.

SHOW ME THE MONEY

A Day Off Would Be Good

In 1918, waitresses at Regina's Balmoral Café went on strike. Their demands were modest:

1. Increase their wages to $5 per day.

2. Decrease their workday from 15 hours to 10.

3. Get at least one day off per week.

Labour Intensive

In 1944 the CCF government passed the Trade Union Act, which guaranteed for the first time anywhere in North America the right of government employees to organize into trade unions and bargain with their employers.

DID YOU KNOW?

The Weyburn Security Bank once issued its own currency. It was accepted in local markets.

Sawbuck Scarcity

In the years before toonies were minted, it was rare to get a $2 bill in your change in Saskatchewan—though they were prevalent in other provinces. Rumour had it that during the '30s, a visit to a Skatchie hooker cost $2, and therefore the bill had a stigma attached. Apparently, $2 bills are considered bad luck in various jurisdictions throughout North America.

Give Me Back My Card

The first automatic teller machine (ATM) in Canada made its debut at the Sherwood Credit Union in Regina. The team who designed it also pioneered the first in-store debit machine at Swift Current's Pioneer Co-op store. Canada now has the highest per-capita use of debit cards in the world.

He Autographed Your Fin

Gerald Bouey of Axford served two seven-year terms as the Governor of the Bank of Canada.

A Little West of Bay Street

The First Nations Bank of Canada is the first chartered bank in Canada with headquarters in Saskatoon. The bank has branches in four provinces and the Yukon Territory.

ENTREPRENEURS

Reeling in Some Serious Dough

Len Thompson of Abernethy was a World War I vet and a farmer who loved to fish. In 1929, he started a fishing lure manufacturing company, which created the legendary "Five of Diamonds" lure and the classic "Red and White."

The Ham Man

In 1940, Fred Mendel of Saskatoon started Intercontinental Packers, which became one of Canada's "Big Five" meat packers. Initially the company shipped canned ham to the U.S., leading *Time* magazine to dub Mendel "the Ham Man." Mendel was the only Saskatchewan resident to receive the Canadian Industrial Development Award. He was an avid art collector and patron, and the 'Tooner's Mendel Art Gallery is named after him.

Amazing Grace

Grace Fletcher of Saskatoon was one of the province's early tycoons. She sold railway carloads of buffalo bones to the U.S., plus she ran a general store, a livery stable and a land agency.

DID YOU KNOW?

Jean Louis Legare of Willow Bunch set up a cheese factory in the 1880s—making cheese manufacturing one of Saskatchewan's first industries.

Believe It Or Not

Jimmy Pattison, who was born in Saskatoon, was listed as number 194 on the 2006 Forbes list of the world's richest people. Chairman, president, CEO, and sole owner of the third-largest,

privately held company in Canada, Pattison owns, among other things, numerous car dealerships, Overwaitea, Save-On-Foods, radio and television stations, and the "Ripley's Believe It Or Not" franchise. He got his start by selling garden seeds when he was 12.

The Great Saskatchewan Centennial Fowl Supper

Leonard Lee, originally of Algrove and a graduate of a one-room school in Archerwill, is the founder and owner of the successful garden and woodworking tool company, Lee Valley Tools. Although he hadn't lived in Saskatchewan for almost five decades, as the province's 100th birthday approached, Lee found himself looking for a way to celebrate. So, in Ottawa on September 2, 2005, Lee hosted a fowl supper for Saskatchewan expatriates. Nearly 300 people attended, including prominent Skatchies such as former premier Allen Blakeney, former MP Bill McKnight, and TV journalist Pamela Wallin. Guests participated in a number of contests, including one for writing the best Saskatchewan limerick. They also enjoyed perogies and saskatoon berry pie.

THE POLS

In Saskatchewan, politics comes as naturally as breathing the prairie air. And the province is often ahead of the curve when it comes to vision. Must be all that wide open space...

The Greatest Canadian

As Saskatchewan's seventh and longest-serving premier, T.C. Douglas led the first socialist government in North America. A founder and leader of the CCF, and the first federal leader of the NDP, Douglas transformed the role of government in Saskatchewan and across the country. He's perhaps best known as "the father of Medicare."

Still Crazy About Tommy After All These Years

In 2004, Canadians were asked to vote for the "Greatest Canadian" for a CBC-TV program of the same name. In a field crowded with (mostly) worthy candidates, Tommy Douglas emerged the winner. The rest of the top ten (in descending order) were:

- Terry Fox
- Pierre Elliott Trudeau
- Sir Frederick Banting
- Dr. David Suzuki
- Lester Pearson
- Don Cherry
- Sir John A. Macdonald
- Alexander Graham Bell
- Wayne Gretzky

Other figures with Saskatchewan connections in the Top 100 included Louis Riel (number 11), John Diefenbaker (47), Sandra Schmirler (81) and Joni Mitchell (93).

Watch Out for the Little Fellow with an Idea

When Douglas was elected premier of Saskatchewan in 1944 (the CCF won 47 of 53 seats), he set out to implement what was considered a radical and ambitious program. He passed more than 100 bills in his first term, creating Crown corporations that brought electricity, paved roads and phone service to rural areas. The CCF also introduced publicly owned auto insurance, advanced labour legislation, a program to offer free hospital care to all citizens, free school textbooks, debt relief for farmers and a Saskatchewan Bill of Rights.

A Leg Up

Douglas' vision for universal health care began when he was a 10-year-old boy in Winnipeg and had to be hospitalized for a leg infection. As his working-class family had no money for a specialist, doctors said the only option was to amputate the leg. Luckily, a visiting surgeon offered to operate on Douglas for free and saved the limb. Douglas recognized at that tender age that no one's health care should depend on his or her ability to pay for it.

Red Scare

It was revealed in 2006 that the RCMP had had spies shadowing Tommy Douglas for more than three decades. Mounties monitored his speeches, eavesdropped on conversations and filed lengthy reports on his activities. Douglas, who probably suspected he was being watched, once said, "Setting people to spy on one another is not the way to protect freedom."

Some Quick Facts about Tommy

- ☞ He was born in Falkirk, Scotland.

- ☞ In 1922, Douglas won the Manitoba Lightweight Boxing Championship title.

- ☞ He invested in Regina's first drive-in theatre but sold his share when opposition members nicknamed it "the premier's passion pit."

- ☞ While working as a Baptist preacher in Weyburn, Douglas completed two degrees by correspondence. His M.A. thesis dealt with eugenics, a theory he later repudiated.

- ☞ Douglas' nickname in Weyburn was "Slivers," given to him after he sat on a wooden bench in his swimming trunks.

- ☞ At the outbreak of World War II, Douglas enlisted and was headed for the Winnipeg Grenadiers when he failed the medical exam due to his childhood leg injury. More than 50 percent of the men in that regiment were killed or wounded in Hong Kong in December 1941.

- ☞ When Douglas and the CCF first took office in 1944, Saskatchewan was $178 million in debt—the equivalent of over $15 billion today!

- ☞ He was struck by a bus in 1984 but recovered quickly. (Lester Pearson was also once hit by a bus. Hmm.)

- During a 1960's demonstration on Parliament Hill, a man started to swing a two-by-four at a woman. Douglas stepped in and wrestled it away from the attacker.

- And of course, T.C. Douglas is the father of Shirley Douglas, noted actress. Shirley was once refused a work permit in the U.S. due to her support of Black Panther causes, and she continues to be politically active today, particularly in the fight to preserve Medicare. Shirley was once married to actor Donald Sutherland.

- Which brings us to Tommy Douglas's grandson, Keifer Sutherland, star of the very popular TV series *24*!

DID YOU  KNOW?

Tommy Douglas' favourite snacks were raisin pie and raisin toast.

A Few Words from Tommy

- On free enterprise: "It's every man for himself the elephant said when he danced among the chickens."

- In response to Premier James Gardiner's accusation that Douglas is "no farmer": "No, and I never laid an egg either, but I know more about omelettes than most hens."

- On choosing between the Tories and the Liberals: "It's like having to choose between being hanged or shot."

- "I never thought a man could save his soul if his belly was empty."

- "Man can fly in the air like a bird, swim under the ocean like a fish, he can burrow into the ground like a mole. Now if he could only walk the earth like a man, this would be paradise."

☛ "I was a printer and then I became a preacher. Then I became a politician and then I became a premier. And that is the true descent of man."

☛ Tommy's most famous story is "Mouseland," which is about the mice who keep choosing to elect either a white cat or a black cat, and whose lives are constantly miserable and oppressed no matter which type of cat is in power. Finally a mouse suggests electing a government made up of mice. The other mice accuse him of being a Communist and send him to jail. Douglas always ended the story by saying, "But I want to remind you that you can lock up a mouse or a man…but you can't lock up an idea."

DIEFENBAKER

Dief Will Be the Chief Again

John George Diefenbaker was born in Ontario but moved as a boy to a homestead near Borden, in the Prince Albert area. Diefenbaker became Canada's 13th prime minister (1957–63), the first westerner to hold the office. "Dief," a charismatic and larger-than-life figure, championed "one Canada" and was a ferocious supporter of human rights at home and around the world.

Dief and Laurier

On July 29, 1910, Diefenbaker was a 15-year-old paperboy in Saskatoon, where Prime Minister Wilfrid Laurier had just arrived to lay the cornerstone of the University of Saskatchewan. As Diefenbaker approached the train station, he spotted Laurier's private car and the prime minister himself out on the platform "taking the air." Laurier gave the boy a quarter, and the two had a talk about Canada. Each must have impressed the other, for later that day Laurier mentioned his chat with the newsboy in his public remarks. He noted that Diefenbaker had broken off the encounter, saying, "Sorry Prime Minister, I can't waste any more time on you, I've got work to do."

The southeast corner of 21st Street and 1st Avenue South is now known as "Diefenbaker Corner," and a statue commemorating the meeting between the two prime ministers stands there.

Sixth Time Lucky

Dief was defeated in his first five tries at running for public office. One of the defeats was in 1926 at the hands of Prime Minister Mackenzie King, who had parachuted into the Prince Albert riding.

Nostradamus Couldn't Have Done Better

Dief took part in the "Mock Parliament" while he was a student at the University of Saskatchewan. *The Sheaf* campus newspaper noted his "zeal" and predicted that in 40 years he'd be the Leader of the Opposition in the House of Commons. The prediction was only off by one year!

Diefenbaker for the Defense

Dief was a criminal lawyer and defended many accused murderers. During a case in 1956, Diefenbaker tried to prove his client's innocence by acting out what had happened at the murder scene and flinging himself across the courtroom. The judge said, "Mr. Diefenbaker, if you will come out from underneath the table I will be able to follow your argument more closely."

Surprise!

In 1957 Diefenbaker's Tories formed a minority government, to the surprise of many political observers. The following year, Dief's party won the biggest majority ever recorded, with 208 seats, a majority of votes, and seats in 9 out of 10 provinces. (Brian Mulroney's Tories broke this record in 1984 by winning 211 seats.)

Air Rage

A few days after winning the 1957 election, Dief and his wife Olive took a plane back to Ottawa. Upon learning that Air Canada had lost his luggage, Dief reportedly pitched a fit in the airport, yelling "Don't they know who I am?!"

Howdy, Pontiff

During a conversation with Pope John XXIII, Diefenbaker asked him, "How does it feel to be the Pope anyhow?" His Holiness replied, "Well, here I am near the end of the road and at the top of the heap."

Camelot vs. Prairie Populism

Dief didn't get along nearly so well with John F. Kennedy, his American counterpart in the early 1960s. Kennedy got off on the wrong foot with Diefenbaker by pronouncing his surname "Diefenbawwwker." And after their first meeting, where they chatted about fishing, JFK reportedly said, "I don't want to see that boring S.O.B. again."

There's some evidence to suggest that Jack Kennedy worked behind the scenes to ensure Dief's defeat in 1963.

Meal Fit for a Princess

Olive Diefenbaker made this chicken salad for Princess Margaret when she came to visit at Harrington Lake:

Combine:
10 cups (2 L) chicken, cooked and diced
10 tsp. (130 mL) lemon juice
5 cups (1 L) diced celery
2½ cups (575 mL) seedless grapes
10 hard-boiled eggs, sliced
3 cups (700 mL) blanched almonds
2½ cups (575 mL) of mayonnaise

Double, Double, Diefenbubble

The Chief's surname troubled him all his life—and he was not amused by some of its permutations. Over the years "Diefenbaker" gave rise to:

- "Diefenbuck" or "Diefendollar" to describe his government's devalued currency. (There was a great outcry when, in 1962, the Canadian dollar sank to 92.5 cents American!)

- "Diefenbunker" to describe the 30,000-square-metre bunker built during his reign that was meant to be the last refuge of Canada's political and military elites in the case of a nuclear war.

☛ And Dief swore that once, a BC car salesman introduced him as "John Studebaker"!

Some Quick Facts about the Chief

☛ He could read approximately 300 pages per hour.

☛ He described himself as "a teetotaller but not a prohibitionist," though his wife Olive maintained he occasionally drank a glass of sherry.

☛ Dief won 13 elections and was returned to the House of Commons for 39 uninterrupted years.

☛ Stringband's song "Dief Will Be the Chief Again" was inspired by a conversation folksinger Bob Bossin had with Ontario premier Bob Rae. Dief himself once reviewed the song, saying, "As a connoisseur of good music, I am simply delighted."

- He was inducted into the Blood tribe as "Chief Many Spotted Horses," perhaps because he once intervened personally to save 250 wild ponies on Sable Island.

- Dief opposed the adoption of the 1965 Canadian red maple leaf flag, referring to it as "Pearson's folly."

- Dief was the only Canadian prime minister to have been a Shriner.

- He never received the Order of Canada, since sitting politicians are not eligible, and Dief was a member of the House of Commons from his first election until his death.

- It's estimated that Dief's funeral cost $485,000, the most expensive send-off for any politician in Canadian history.

DID YOU  KNOW?

One of Dief's heroes was Sir John A. Macdonald, Canada's first prime minister. Dief collected Macdonald memorabilia throughout his life.

In His Name

Although Diefenbaker always felt that his road in life would have been easier had he not been saddled with such an "ethnic" surname, it has been adopted by:

- Lake Diefenbaker, the reservoir created following the construction of the Gardiner Dam on the South Saskatchewan River

- The John G. Diefenbaker Airport in Saskatoon

- The Diefenbaker Centre at the University of Saskatchewan, where Dief served as chancellor

- Schools in Ontario, Alberta and Saskatchewan

- A hill trail connecting two battle sites of Israel's 1948 war of independence

- A planet in the "BattleTech Wargame" universe

- And the television show *Due South* featured a deaf, doughnut-snatching police dog named "Diefenbaker"!

Resting Place

Diefenbaker died on August 16, 1979, in Ottawa. His body was transported from Ottawa to Saskatoon by train, and thousands of people lined the tracks to say farewell to "the Chief." Jon Vickers sang at the service, which was attended by Prime Minister Joe Clark and Premier Allen Blakeney, among other dignitaries.

In his will, Dief had specified that the Canadian flag be draped over his coffin—and then covered by the Red Ensign that he had championed in Parliament. Mr. Diefenbaker and his late wife Olive were buried on the grounds of the Right Honourable John G. Diefenbaker Centre for the Study of Canada. Some Saskatonians say that on dark nights the Chief's ghost can be glimpsed there, on the grassy bank overlooking the South Saskatchewan River…

GABRIEL DUMONT

One of the most romantic figures in Saskatchewan's history, Dumont has inspired generations of Métis. He was a consummate man of the prairie, elected as the permanent chief of the Métis buffalo hunters when he was only 25 years old. A good shot and a natural horseman, Dumont spoke six languages. He foresaw great changes coming for his people and was determined to act on their behalf.

In 1872 Dumont opened a small store, a billiards hall and a ferry upstream from Batoche, and the following year was elected the president of the first local government between Manitoba

and the Rockies. Throughout the 1870s and '80s Dumont pressed the federal government for redress and protection for his people. When negotiations failed, and Louis Riel declared a provisional government at Batoche, Dumont became the military commander in charge of the Métis army of only 300. Although he won battles against the NWMP at Duck Lake and against General Middleton's army at Fish Creek, the Rebellion was defeated. Dumont fled to America, but later returned to Batoche, where he died, in 1906.

Quick Facts and Rumours about Dumont

☞ After escaping to the U.S., Gabriel Dumont joined Buffalo Bill Cody's Wild West Show. Billed as "The Prince of the Plains," Dumont's sharpshooter act was a hit in towns throughout America.

☞ Madeleine Dumont, Gabriel's wife, is believed to have travelled alone from Batoche to Winnipeg to sell furs while her husband was occupied with Métis affairs. She helped to run the ferry service at "Gabriel's Crossing."

☞ Dumont plotted to rescue Louis Riel from jail, but Riel was too carefully guarded, and the escape was never attempted.

☞ The young John Diefenbaker met Gabriel Dumont after he returned to the Batoche area. Dief said that even as an old man, Dumont could still throw a tin can in the air and shoot it twice on the way down. He also speculated that the perfect centre part in Dumont's hair was an after-effect of having had his head grazed by a bullet at Duck Lake.

☞ Dumont could speak several languages, including Cree, English, French, and three or four dialects common to plains tribes.

- Famed for his skills as a guerilla fighter, a guide, an interpreter and a buffalo hunter, Dumont was also known to be a pretty sharp gambler.

- Legend has it that Dumont is buried standing up in the Batoche cemetery. The rumour is that he's upright and facing the South Saskatchewan—because the river is the one thing that the white man couldn't change. His grave is marked with a large triangular slab of rock.

- Dumont's name lives on: The Gabriel Dumont Institute of Native Studies and Research with campuses in Regina, Saskatoon and Prince Albert; the Dumont Bridge near Rosthern; a French first-language high school in London, Ontario; and a Saskatoon park.

DID YOU KNOW?

Although he could neither read nor write, in his later years Dumont dictated two books about his life.

POLITICAL POTPOURRI

Party On!

The following political parties are currently registered in Saskatchewan. (Only the first two hold seats in the Legislature.)

- New Democratic Party of Saskatchewan
- Saskatchewan Party
- Saskatchewan Liberal Party
- Conservative Party of Saskatchewan
- Western Independence Party of Saskatchewan
- Saskatchewan Marijuana Party
- Green Party of Saskatchewan
- Saskatchewan Heritage Party

Wasn't that a Party?

Here are some parties once active:

- Progressive Party
- Co-operative Commonwealth Federation
- Labor-Progressive Party
- Social Credit Party of Saskatchewan
- First Nations Party of Saskatchewan
- Non-Partisan League
- Unionest Party

I Am Woman, Hear Me Vote

Women got the right to vote in Saskatchewan on March 14, 1916.

Sheet-Heads

In 1926, American Klansmen came to Saskatchewan, playing on Anglo-Saxon Protestant fears by spreading wild rumours about Roman Catholic and non-English-speaking immigrants, and spouting prejudice against Natives and Jews. Within a year, the KKK had recruited an estimated 10,000 members in the province, giving it the dubious distinction of having the largest per-capita Klan membership in North America. A rally in Moose Jaw in July 1927 drew a crowd of over 7000. The Klan even became an election issue for Premier James Gardiner and Conservative leader J.T.M. Anderson in 1929. Thankfully, by the mid-1930s, Saskatchewan's Klan chapters had disintegrated.

DID YOU  KNOW?

In 1883, Prince Albert citizens got so furious over a dispute about where to build a telegraph line that they burned two public figures in effigy.

Nothing to Lose But Their Chains

The "Regina Manifesto" was the programme adopted by the CCF at their first national convention in 1933. The plan called for the nationalization of transportation, communications, electrical power and other services. It advocated a planned economy and a national banking system, and called for a National Labour Code that would include insurance for illness, old age and unemployment. It also proposed social service programs such as health care.

The manifesto remained the official program of the CCF until 1956—when prevailing anti-communist attitudes led the party to back off the stance that the CCF "not rest content until it has eradicated capitalism."

God Save the King

The 1939 visit of King George VI and Queen Elizabeth drew thousands of people to the royal train's whistle stops across the province. Melville painted a greeting on its grain elevator, and 60,000 people descended on the town!

Wise Guys

About 20 senior public servants left Saskatchewan for Ottawa in 1964, after the election of Ross Thatcher. The "Saskatchewan Mafia," as they were named, were hired by Lester Pearson and influenced federal policy for many years afterwards.

Tri-Partisanship

In a glorious display of political even-handedness, the dam on the South Saskatchewan River is named for Liberal Premier James Gardiner, the lake is named for Conservative Prime Minister John Diefenbaker, and the surrounding park is named for NDP icon Tommy Douglas. Lake Diefenbaker supplies 50 percent of Saskatchewan with drinking water.

Peace, Man

Saskatchewan produced more than its fair share of peace activists in the politically charged 1960s. In the early part of the decade, leading members of Combined Universities Campaign for Nuclear Disarmament (CUCND) lived cooperatively at "Humanity House" in Saskatoon. Students Union for Peace Action, the main Canadian activist organization, had more Saskatchewan members, per capita, than Toronto ones. In 1967,

1000 University of Regina students boycotted classes to attend a "teach-in." And the Committee to Aid American War Immigrants in that city raised funds for several years to help run two hostels for Vietnam War deserters.

Power to the People

Saskatchewan's Native Action Committee ran a "red power" candidate in the Meadow Lake constituency in the 1968 federal election: Carol Lavallee of the Cowesses Reserve. Black Panthers' luminary Fred Hampton met with Native activists in Saskatchewan and Alberta in November 1969. Famous for saying, "You can jail the revolutionary, but you can't jail the revolution; you can murder a liberator, but you can't murder liberation," Hampton was murdered by Illinois state police about a month after his visit to Canada.

Ahead of Their Time
At a provincial NDP convention in 1967, delegates from Prince Albert made a motion that housewives be paid a salary.

No Shrinking Violet

For almost 40 years, Violet McNaughton of Saskatoon wrote a biweekly column for *The Western Producer,* in which she often discussed controversial topics such as birth control. McNaughton was the first woman elected to the Saskatchewan Grain Growers Association, and she fought for women's enfranchisement.

Secret Life
Saskatchewan's first premier, T. Walter Scott, was born in Ontario—to an unmarried woman. Although this is not uncommon today, in 1905, when Scott took office, being born out of wedlock was considered scandalous. Scott was a popular premier who won three elections—but sadly, he suffered from depression and died in a mental institution.

Feathering the Unionest

In 1980, Dick Collver, a former leader of Saskatchewan's Progressive Conservative Party, formed the "Unionest" party, which was dedicated to uniting the four western provinces. Conservative Dennis Ham joined him, and this made the two Unionests the official third party in the Legislature. The duo then qualified for $56,000 in additional funding!

The NDP quickly introduced retroactive legislation that disqualified the Unionests; the party soon sputtered out and

Collver retired to a ranch in Arizona. Ham is the brother of Lynda Haverstock, who later became the leader of the Saskatchewan Liberal Party and the province's lieutenant-governor.

Monkeying Around

Amadee Forget, Saskatchewan's first lieutenant-governor (1901–10), had a pet spider monkey named "Jocko." Forget kept a tiny rocking chair for the monkey in his office.

Break a Leg in Those New Shoes
Ralph Goodale, the Liberal finance minister originally from Wilcox, made his acting debut on an episode of *Corner Gas* on November 14, 2005—the same day he presented a new federal budget.

Purse Strings

The first woman in Canada to hold a minister of finance position was Janice MacKinnon, who was Skatchie minister of finance from 1993 to 1997.

Father Bob

In 1977, the NDP approached popular Saskatoon parish priest Father Bob Ogle to run in the federal election. Ogle had been a missionary in northeastern Brazil for six years and had written a book about global social justice, but his candidacy wasn't given much chance to succeed—his opponent was the popular Liberal transport minister, Otto Lang.

On his bicycle, Ogle canvassed every house in the constituency, and in 1979, he defeated Lang and went off to Ottawa. In 1984, however, the Vatican decided priests should not be allowed to run for public office, and Father Bob retired from politics.

Sylvia Again

Sylvia Fedoruk, born in Canora, keeps popping up in various categories of this book! A remarkably talented research scientist and a member of the Saskatchewan Sports Hall of Fame, Fedoruk was also Saskatchewan's first female lieutenant-governor! She served in the post from 1988 to 1994.

Madame Sauve

Jeanne Sauve, born in Prud'homme, was Canada's first female governor general. She was also the first female Speaker of the House of Commons.

Two in a Row

The governor general who succeeded Jeanne Sauve was Ray Hnatyshyn of Saskatoon. Hnatyshyn hosted a 1992 rock concert at Rideau Hall known as "His Excellency's Most Excellent Rock Concert." He also established the Governor General's Awards for the Performing Arts. In 2004 the government issued a post-age stamp in his honour.

STRANGE DOINGS

*Beyond this is another dimension—a dimension of sound,
a dimension of sight, a dimension of mind. You're moving into
a land of both shadow and substance, of things and ideas. You've
just crossed over into—the Saskatchewan Zone...*

Where's the Pied Piper When You Need Him?

In the summer of 2005, a plague of deer mice descended on the Lacadena/Elrose/Kindersley area. Windbreaks appeared to be moving as mice swarmed over the caragana branches. Farmers who fashioned traps from five-gallon pails found the pails filled to the brim with mice every morning. In Eston a group of farmers counted 300 dead mice under one sheet of plywood. And cars on the highway between Eston and Rosetown slipped and slid on the road surface, which had become slick with mouse guts.

Then suddenly, the little vermin began to die off, victims of a mousy virus. In fields near Kindersley, dead rodents were piled up like snowdrifts. Reportedly, residents in the affected areas still can't watch certain Disney cartoons without shuddering.

The Circle Game

Saskatchewan is Canada's crop circle hotspot, according to the Canadian Crop Circles Research Network (CCCRN), which monitors the bizarre phenomenon. Almost 40 percent of all crop circles reported in the country are in Saskatchewan. And if there were a crop circle capital of Canada, the town of Midale would win, hands-down—at least seven crop circles were found there in 2001 alone!

The mysterious designs include elaborate patterns of interlocking rings, dumbbells, hexagrams, "Xs" and, as in the case of a formation near the Dinsmore Hutterite Brethren Colony,

something that looked suspiciously like the ancient symbol for "female." While cynics claim crop circles are made by farmers with too much time on their hands, others speculate that radiation, magnetic force or plant disease are responsible. Gord Sopczak of the CCCRN thinks they're messages from another dimension, urging us to "focus on the higher love vibrations." Who could argue with that?

Crop Circle Reports, by Province and Territory, 1925–2006

Saskatchewan	103
Ontario	42
Alberta	32
Manitoba	27
British Columbia	22
Québec	13
Northwest Territories	3
New Brunswick	2
Prince Edward Island	2
Nova Scotia	1

Move Over, Stonehenge

Near Cypress Hills Interprovincial Park is a weird rock formation that's been puzzling scientists for decades. Huge, grey, loaf-
shaped stones—some with carvings, some with holes drilled in
them—are arranged on range of hills. A message from outer
space? A lost civilization?

Rock and Roll

Near the Big Muddy village of St. Victor, an amazing array of
ancient petroglyphs can be seen in sections of sandstone at the
top of a cliff. The symbols include a grizzly bear claw, human
footprints and handprints, bison hoofprints, and other animal
and human depictions. The incredible images are best seen at
certain times of day—one human figure, which looks full-faced
and healthy in the morning light, appears skeleton-like in the
evening. No one is sure who the carvers were, or how long ago
the symbols were carved, but they are an eerily beautiful art
form and a mysterious glimpse of life in ancient times.

Boulder to Boulder

Several boulder monuments have been recorded in
Saskatchewan—167 to be exact. Medicine wheels are ancient
stone structures arranged in patterns that look like wagon
wheels, and they were probably used for rituals or as "sky calen-
dars." Many seem to be in alignment not only with celestial
bodies but also with each other. Medicine wheels can still be
seen at many Saskatchewan locations, including Oxbow,
Hughton, Frenchman River, Moose Mountain, and of course
at Wanuskewin Heritage Park outside Saskatoon.

An unusual animal effigy near Minton in Big Muddy country
is in the shape of a 40-metre turtle. And in a field near Cabri
Lake, large boulders are arranged in the outline of a human.
The anatomically correct man measures about 8.5 metres from
head to toe, with a width of approximately 4.5 metres, and can
only be properly seen from the air.

Twisted!

If you go down to the woods today, be sure to avoid the ones in the Thickwood Hills near Mayfair. Nicknamed "The Crooked Trees" by local residents, a grove of aspens on Skip and Linda Magowan's farm looks like the haunted forest from the movie *The Headless Horseman*—branches loop, twist and snake around in every direction, creating a dark and ominous overhead canopy. Local stories place the responsibility for the mutant forest on everything from Shetland pony–sized jackrabbits nibbling on tree shoots to aliens peeing on the spot…and so far plant breeders from the University of Saskatchewan have been unable to come up with a more scientific explanation.

Loch Turtle Monster

About once a year, a saucer-eyed fisherman boots it back to the shore of Turtle Lake babbling about a frightening encounter with something scaly from the deeps. Eyewitnesses say it's a creature somewhere between 3 and 9 metres long, with a head like a seahorse. Or maybe a pig.

A few residents of the resort community northwest of North Battleford think the "monster" is only a giant sturgeon. But the creature's been there as long as anyone can remember—and one theory holds that a family of plesiosaurs is lurking somewhere far below the surface of the deceptively calm body of water.

The Thing from Deep Cove

In "Deep Cove," a part of Reindeer Lake formed by a meteorite strike, dark water supposedly hides a monster that regularly breaks through the ice to pull caribou down to the murky depths.

Sasquatchewan

In December 2006, a woman from the northern community of Deschambault Lake was convinced that she saw a sasquatch by the side of the highway. She described it as a large, hairy creature, not bearlike, that walked upright. Several men from the village found footprints and a tuft of hair in the area.

Hail Mary

In the fall of 2002, images of the Virgin Mary began appearing in a greenhouse in the northern Saskatchewan community of Ile-A-La-Crosse. On September 8—the Blessed Virgin's official birthday—the holy mother appeared in "condensation" between two sealed panes of glass. The elderly greenhouse owner tried to scrub it away, but the image kept reappearing.

Witnesses reported a strong scent of roses and a warming of the air each time the phenomenon began. The apparitions were detailed, brightly coloured as if lit from within and varied in size from 15 centimetres to 1.5 metres. The visions recurred every evening for several weeks, and more than 7000 visitors flooded the remote community to see them. "It was the most beautiful moment of my life," said one young observer.

GHOST STORIES

Ghost Dance

Strange things go on at the Moose Head Inn at Kenosee Lake.... When Dale Orsted bought the nightclub in 1990, he moved into the apartment upstairs. At first he was only bothered by small objects that went missing, but then, late at night, he'd be woken up by loud banging on the outside walls and doors. RCMP investigated several times, but found no burglars.

Then Orsted started to do some renovating, and things really got weird. In the middle of the night, Dale and his girlfriend heard what sounded like cars crashing in the bar downstairs. The manifestation created enough physical impact that dishes sitting in the sink broke, mops and pails started flying across the dance floor, and the doors of the stalls in the women's washroom swung open and shut without being touched. Sometimes, giving "last call" was unnecessary because the heavy double security doors would fly wide open and slam shut—patrons usually took the hint and fled!

Sing Me No Sad Songs

Mary Trivett and her husband came to homestead near Readlyn, Saskatchewan, in 1908. Originally from England, Mary had been a staunch Salvation Army member, but since there was no Sally Ann near Readlyn, she joined the United Church congregation. She once confessed to the organist, Walter Eaglestone, that she missed the upbeat music of the Salvation Army, which was full of drums and tambourines. "When I go," she told him, "I don't want the organ played at my funeral." Eaglestone dismissed the comment, for there were few other musical options in their area at the time.

When Mary Trivett died in the spring of 1928, Walter prepared a number of hymns for her funeral. However, as the mourners started filling the church, the organ refused to play. Eaglestone examined the instrument, found nothing wrong, and tried again. No sound could be produced no matter what he did. Finally he gave up, and the funeral service was conducted without music. After the interment Walter Eaglestone went back to the church and tried the organ again. It worked perfectly.

DID YOU KNOW?

Government House in Regina, built in 1881 and location of the offices of the lieutenant-governor, is home to a mischievous ghost dubbed "Howie." Howie seems content to flush the occasional toilet, open a door now and then or sometimes do a bit of cleaning and polishing.

Cold Case

Stories about eerie happenings often circulated through the tiny village of Bickleigh, now a—no pun intended—ghost town. During the 1930s, '40s and '50s, tales about spectral horsemen galloping by or reports of ghostly footsteps were well known to locals.

In 1982, a farmer found a human skull while cultivating his field, about one kilometre from where the railway tracks had once run past Bickleigh. Further digging turned up leg, arm and rib bones. Scientists ascertained that the remains were approximately 60 years old. It's thought the bones may have belonged to a railway worker who disappeared from the area in 1924.

Will o' the Wisp
"Ghost lights" have been seen at graveyards throughout the province. A ghost light starts near the ground, is blue and about the size of a ping-pong ball, then grows larger and turns orange as it rises. Candle Lake, near Prince Albert, is said to have been

named for the ghost lights that appear on the northern end of the lake near old Native graves. And the Tabor Cemetery near Esterhazy is haunted by a globe of fiery light so persistent that it's known as "Old Faithful."

Old Wives Lake

The legend of Old Wives Lake has been passed down through generations of Plains Natives. The tale holds that a raiding party of Blackfoot were after a tribe of Assiniboine. Three elderly Assiniboine grandmothers offered to stay behind to keep the fire burning, to fool the Blackfoot while the others made their escape. When the attackers found only the old ladies on site, they were furious. The women ran as far as the shore, then drowned as they tried to swim to the other side. Ever since, when the wind blows, the mocking laughter of the grandmothers can be heard. Today the lake itself is gone, and only a desolate alkali flat remains…but residents testify that the eerie voices linger on.

Ghost Bussers
In Saskatoon, a group of volunteers runs a late-night bus tour of spooky sights, including the haunted Marr House on 11th Street near Victoria; the Diefenbaker Centre, which is haunted by the Chief himself; and the road to the dump, where a teenaged girl with dripping wet hair has been known to flag down passing cars…and then vanish.

Spirited
Fort San, the old tuberculosis sanatorium near Fort Qu'Appelle, is arguably the most haunted place in Saskatchewan. Opened in 1919, the San was home to the gravely ill and dying for many years, until the advent of antibiotics made tuberculosis less common and less lethal. In the 1970s and '80s, the Saskatchewan Summer School of the Arts operated at the site, offering workshops in art, music, drama and writing. Dozens of workshop

participants had strange and inexplicable experiences during their time at the San. Ghostly nurses were seen folding linens beside cupboards, transparent patients in old-fashioned clothing appeared near beds, lights flicked on and off at random, and creaky wheelchairs were heard scraping down the halls.

One group of respected writers experimented with a Ouija board and were so terrified by what happened that they don't even like to talk about it. An award-winning poet was apparently flung across the room by unseen forces. "It was as if," said one participant, "we had opened a portal to hell."

Ghost Train

On a stretch of railway tracks near the village of St. Louis, generations of residents have seen the "Ghost Train." A light, large and brilliant, appears to come rocketing right down the railway line. The ghostly beam has been known to pass straight through anyone brave enough to stand in its path—and to disappear a split-second later.

IT CAME FROM OUTER SPACE

E.T., Phone Langenburg

On the morning of September 1, 1974, farmer Edwin Fuhr was harvesting his canola crop when he noticed a metallic, dome-shaped object in a grassy area. As he approached it, he noticed it was spinning. Looking around, Fuhr spotted four more identical objects hovering in a semi-circle above the ground. As Fuhr watched, one seemed to probe the ground. Suddenly it took off, followed by the others, each emitting a puff of grey vapour.

RCMP investigated and found five rings of depressed grass. Fuhr described the "flying saucers" as made of highly polished metal with a "brushed" finish. Each was about 1.5 metres high at the peak.

Close Encounter of the Nipawin Kind

In the early summer of 1935 near Nipawin, a young woman and two men saw an oval-shaped object supported by six legs sitting in the muskeg. For half an hour they watched as a dozen or so small creatures in silver suits went up and down a ladder attached to the object. Square imprints and a burnt mark were left behind.

Midale Again?!

And on February 21, 2005, a couple in Midale saw a huge, oval, silver object with a green glow surrounding it, travelling at high speed past their bedroom window. Transmissions from the nearby SaskTel radio tower were knocked out for two days.

THIS AND THAT

And now for something completely different! A veritable olio of facts, figures and sheer silliness that defies categorization!

Saskatchewan Glossary

Biffy:	bathroom, as in *The Biffy Book of Saskatchewan Trivia*
Boh:	Molson's Bohemian beer
Bunnyhug:	hooded sweatshirt
Butte:	hill
Butterfly:	dance (popular at weddings) involving three dancers linking arms and a lot of twirling
Calved:	quit, usually referring to a vehicle or implement
Coulees:	valleys
Gibbled:	broken, wobbly or dysfunctional; the term originated from an employee of a Wynyard chicken-processing plant who mispronounced "giblets"
Gitch:	undies, tighty whities
Half-ton:	pick-up truck
Nuisance grounds:	the dump (somewhat out of fashion; may be replaced by "the lower mall")
Pil:	Pilsner beer
Pull beer:	to buy beer on behalf of underage drinkers
Slough:	pond-like body of water
Sucking slough water:	extremely tired
Vi-co:	chocolate milk

Welcome Mat

Kyle Macdonald of Montréal started a website and offered to trade one red paper clip for something bigger. His aim was to keep swapping over the course of a year to see what he'd end up with. Macdonald started on July 12, 2005, and made 14 trades for the paper clip:

1. a pen shaped like a fish, for

2. a doorknob that looks like E.T., for

3. a Coleman stove, for

4. a generator, for

5. "An instant party" (Keg of beer, neon beer sign, IOU for a second keg of beer), for

6. Michel Barrette's skidoo, for

7. a trip to Yahk, BC, for

8. a cube van, for

9. a recording contract, for

10. one year's free rent in Phoenix, for

11. an afternoon with Alice Cooper, for

12. a KISS snow globe, for

13. a role in a Corbin Bernsen movie, for...

14. a house at 203 Main Street, Kipling, Saskatchewan, on July 12, 2006!

A huge housewarming party followed. Macdonald has since been named one of VH1's 40 Biggest Internet Stars. He's recently been asked to do a commercial for the Volkswagen Polo, which is to be filmed in Kipling—despite the fact that so far, not one person in Kipling drives a Polo.

Whack-a-Richardson's-Ground-Squirrel Day

On May 1, 1917, schoolchildren all across the province were let out of school for an organized gopher hunt. It was christened "The First Annual Saskatchewan Gopher Day."

Maybe Fred and Barney Were Members

Benevolent societies such as the Elks and the Kinsmen do many good things for Saskatchewan. Earlier more obscure lodges and orders in the province included:

☛ The Loyal Order of Moose

☛ Woodsmen of the World

☛ Royal Templars of Temperance

☛ Sons of Jove

☛ The Royal Antedeluvian Order of Buffaloes

Bingo!

Some Saskatchewanians got lucky on the lottery:

☛ Delmer Struss of Sheho won $16.7 million in a Lotto Super 7 draw in 1996.

☛ In 2005, Dr. Michael Goldren of Wynyard won a Lotto 6/49 draw worth $14.6 million.

☛ Berta Haley of Arborfield had been living with David Thompson for several years when she discovered a 6/49 lottery ticket in her purse that was worth $2.1 million. She quickly dumped Thompson and moved out of their house. After Thompson sued, a judge ruled that Haley had to split her winnings with her former mate—making their breakup a kind of win-win situation.

☛ And Larry Greenbank, a farmer from Wawota, kept a $2 million winning ticket for five months before cashing it in—because he was too busy farming!

The Shirt Off Its Back

A few T-shirt slogans enjoyed by Saskatchewanians:

- ☞ Surf Saskatchewan

- ☞ Saskatchewan's Potholes Are Bigger Than Your Potholes

- ☞ Saskatchewan: Hard to Spell, Easy to Draw

- ☞ It's a Dry Cold

- ☞ Saskatchewan: Through the Straw Curtain

- ☞ Saskatchewan Farmers Are Outstanding in Their Field

- ☞ Saskatchewan: Flat Out Great

- ☞ I'm Famous in Saskatchewan

A Rose by Any Other Name

The top-10 most popular baby names of 2005 in Saskatchewan were:

Boys	Girls
Ethan	Madison
Joshua	Emma
Matthew	Emily
Carter	Olivia
Logan	Hailey
Jacob	Ava
Ashton	Hannah
Liam	Brooklyn
Austin	Chloe
Owen	Abigail

Some Saskatchewan parents are opting to give their offspring more unusual names, however. Number 30 on the 2005 list was the girl's name "Jorja," a variation of "Georgia," perhaps inspired by the actress who plays Sarah Sidle on the television show *CSI,* Jorja Fox. And 17 Saskatchewan baby girls got the name "Nevaeh"—the word "heaven" spelled backwards. Girls also got a lot of names formerly reserved for boys: Skylar, Tristan, Dylan, Hunter, Drew and Emerson.

Boys weren't off the hook: spelling may be a problem for the spate of boys named Kalen, Kalan, Kayden, Kaiden, Caden, Caleb, and Kaleb. "Chance," "Deacon" and "Blaze" also appear on the boys' list.

Fortunately for those parents tempted to christen their tots "Satan" or "Condoleezza," Saskatchewan Health is prevented from registering any names that are offensive or intended for nothing more than shock value.

DID YOU KNOW?

A crater on Mars is named after the village of Tugaske. There must be a story behind it, but unfortunately, no one in Tugaske seems to know how the name got there!

Saskatchewan, Hollywood Style

In 1954, Hollywood made a movie called *Saskatchewan.* It starred Alan Ladd as RCMP officer Salty O'Rourke, and Shelley Winters as his love interest. The movie features fist fights, explosions and canoe chases. Curiously, many outdoor shots include an impressive range of mountains!

Cameo Appearances

☛ In the film *Atlantic City*, Susan Sarandon's character—a clam-shucking, no-nonsense kind of girl—is supposed to be from Saskatchewan.

☛ A joke in *The Muppet Movie* has Kermit and Fozzie heading to Hollywood but ending up in Saskatchewan.

☛ "Saskatchewan" is one of the words in a crossword puzzle in the 1994 Coen brothers classic *The Hudsucker Proxy*.

☛ In *Shut Up and Sing*, Barbara Koppel's 2006 Oscar-winning documentary about the Dixie Chicks, members of the band's entourage are gobsmacked when a staff member suggests touring to Moose Jaw.

Homer, Sweet Homer

In 1991, television's long-running animated sitcom *The Simpsons* featured Homer Simpson watching the CFL draft picks of the Saskatchewan Roughriders on TV. (The CFL draft isn't televised.) And in 2005, Homer and his father start smuggling in prescription drugs from Canada. Their contact gives them a health card and tells them that they can take the card to any pharmacy "and get enough drugs to make Regina look like Saskatoon."

Simpsons' creator Matt Groening has a real Skatchie connection: his father, Homer Groening, was born to Mennonite parents in Main Centre, Saskatchewan, in 1919. Although Homer Groening and Homer Simpson share a first name, the real-life Homer was apparently a hard worker who had no particular fondness for doughnuts.

Novel Approach

☞ In Donna Tartt's *The Secret History,* characters at a New England college are trying to figure out how to avoid the long arm of the law. One character says, "We'll stay in Montréal for a couple of days. Sell the car. Then take the bus to, I don't know, Saskatchewan or something. We'll go to the weirdest place we can find."

☞ Thriller master John LeCarre uses Saskatchewan as a locale for one of his chapters in the book *The Constant Gardener,* but he's a bit vague on details, describing an "eastern" Saskatchewan "town square," which is located "three hours' rail ride out of Winnipeg."

☞ In the 1960's best-selling novel *Hotel* by Arthur Hailey, witnesses speculate that a suspect may have had Saskatchewan licence plates.

Sing a Song of Saskatchewan

Saskatchewan has oft been celebrated in song. Here are a few favourites:

"Cap in Hand": Scottish brothers The Proclaimers brag about being able to pronounce "Saskatchewan" even as they lament English oppression of their homeland.

"Anywhere But Here": Sammy Kershaw compares the temperature in his connubial bedroom to winter in Saskatoon.

"Runnin' Back to Saskatoon": Guess Who's prairie anthem in which they hang out with grease monkeys, playwrights, soil farmers and other dubious types in the title city.

"The Girl from Saskatoon": Johnny Cash alternately freezes and burns for a girl from the 'Tooner. (Cash liked Saskatchewan. He also put "Gravelbourg" into one of his recorded versions of *I've Been Everywhere.*)

"Canadian Idiot": Weird Al Yankovic reveals the Canadian dream: driving a Zamboni in Saskatchewan.

And Some Favourite Lyrics

Canada's wittiest band, The Arrogant Worms, has given us unforgettable songs such as "Jesus' Brother Bob," "Rippy the Gator," "Worst Seat on the Plane" and the classic love song "Heimlich Maneuver." But the one that's the most fun to sing along with is "The Last Saskatchewan Pirate":

"Then I thought, who gives a damn if all the jobs are gone?

I'm gonna be a PIRATE on the river Saskatchewan!!!

'Cause it's a heave-ho, hi-ho, comin' down the plains

Stealin' wheat and barley and all the other grains

And it's a ho-hey, hi-hey, farmers bar yer doors

When you see the Jolly Roger on Regina's mighty shores!"

(Lyrics quoted by permission of The Arrogant Worms: Mike McCormick, Chris Patterson and Trevor Strong. www.arrogant-worms.com)

OK, OK, Here Are the Flat Jokes...

Some well-worn Saskatchewan jokes:

☛ It's so flat in Saskatchewan that you can watch your dog run away for a week. (Or a train coming for three days, etc, etc, etc.)

☛ It's so flat in Saskatchewan, if you stand on a milkcan and look west, you can see the back of your head.
(Source: *Canadian Sayings* by Bill Casselman)

...And One Wind Joke

You can always tell people from Saskatchewan. When the wind stops blowing, they fall over.
(Canadian Sayings, Casselman)

A Thought from Peter

Peter Gzowski, host of CBC Radio's *Morningside,* once said, "Saskatchewan is the heartland of Canada, the most Canadian of all the provinces."

You Live in Saskatchewan
And finally, here's how to tell whether or not you're a Skatchie...

☛ If your local Dairy Queen is closed from September through May, you live in Saskatchewan.

☛ If someone in a Home Depot store offers you assistance, and they don't work there, you live in Saskatchewan.

☛ If "vacation" means going anywhere south of Regina for the weekend, you live in Saskatchewan.

☛ If you measure distance in squares of farm land, you live in Saskatchewan.

- If you know several people who have hit a cow more than once, you live in Saskatchewan.

- If you sometimes wear a toque while riding your Jet-Ski, you live in Saskatchewan.

- If you can drive 120 kilometres per hour through a raging blizzard without flinching, you live in Saskatchewan.

- If you install security lights on your house and garage, but leave both unlocked, you live in Saskatchewan.

- If you design your kid's Halloween costume to fit over a snowsuit, you live in Saskatchewan.

- If you think driving is better in the winter because the potholes are filled with snow, you live in Saskatchewan.

- If you have more hours on your snow blower than kilometres on your car odometer, you live in Saskatchewan.

- If you've had a lengthy telephone conversation with someone who dialed a wrong number, you live in Saskatchewan.

ABOUT THE AUTHOR

Glenda MacFarlane

Glenda was born in tiny Beechy, Saskatchewan, and her heart still calls the town home. Every morning, she checks Beechy's birthday calendar and thinks longingly of the farm. As a girl, her ambition was to read every book in the local library, and she went on to the University of Saskatchewan to study English and drama. Glenda then became a playwright and performer and has also served as the vice-president of the Saskatchewan Writers Guild. She is currently the editor for a series of plays and other drama publications. Her work has appeared in several anthologies, on CBC radio and on stages across the country. These days, Glenda divides her time between Saskatchewan, Toronto and Prince Edward Island along with her partner and three-year-old daughter.